Pauls Toutonghi

DOG GONE

Pauls Toutonghi is a first-generation American. He has been awarded a Pushcart Prize, and he has written for *The New Yorker*, *The New York Times*, *Virginia Quarterly Review*, *Granta*, *Tin House*, and numerous other periodicals. He lives in Oregon, where he teaches at Lewis & Clark College.

paulstoutonghi.wordpress.com

D0029396

Praise for Pauls Toutonghi's

DOG GONE

"A beautifully told story of a lost childhood, and a woman's efforts to make things right with herself, her children, and the world."   —*The Oregonian*

"The story of loss, love and resilience is told by Toutonghi with lots of heart and humor. The book stresses how heroism can assert itself in the little things we do each day."   —*The News & Observer*

"A poignant reminder of the important role dogs often fill as they help their human companions traverse difficult life passages."   —*Library Journal*

"[Toutonghi] takes an intriguing parcel of family lore—the fervid (some would call it obsessive) hunt for a missing pet—and uses it to explore histories of abuse and illness that cloud an otherwise idyllic suburban household. *Dog Gone* is a quick read with a deceptively humble focus: how dogs impact the lives of the humans who care for them."
—*Willamette Week*

ALSO BY PAULS TOUTONGHI

Red Weather
Evel Knievel Days

DOG GONE

A Lost Pet's Extraordinary Journey
and the Family Who Brought Him Home

DOG GONE

PAULS TOUTONGHI

VINTAGE BOOKS
A Division of Penguin Random House LLC
New York

FIRST VINTAGE BOOKS EDITION, APRIL 2017

The Cataloging-in-Publication Data is available from the
Library of Congress.

Vintage Books Trade Paperback ISBN: 978-1-101-97101-7
eBook ISBN: 978-1-101-94702-9

Illustrations by Margaret Owen

www.vintagebooks.com

Printed in the United States of America
10 9 8 7 6 5 4 3 2 1

For all the dogs who never made it back

Contents

Author's Note

Every family, it seems, has that single pet—the one that's different from all the others—the one that somehow becomes enshrined in family lore. It is the most destructive, or the sweetest, or does the single most dramatic thing. Kitchen cabinets are rummaged through, garages are ransacked, duvets are gnawed and shredded. Or great odds are somehow defeated. A car fender does not kill, an illness is overcome, an unusual skill is mastered. There is a profound uniqueness to these animals. They are not human, but that's part of why they are incredible. From within their animal selves, they summon something that confirms their individuality, their vivacity and vigor, their hold on a deep and enduring presence in our hearts and minds. For my extended family—the Marshalls of McLean, Virginia—Gonker was that pet.

Gonker was a golden retriever who—above all things—loved wearing sweater vests. In any room, Gonker refused to sprawl on the floor like a dog, choosing instead to sit in chairs—to perch on benches and bedsides, his paws crossed, his chin lifted. He was regal. But he had his weaknesses, too. An open trash can was a temptation. An unguarded stick of butter? Irresistible. He would, somewhat mysteriously, chase anyone in a white coat. When my mother- and father-in-law, Virginia and John Marshall, first told me the story of how Gonker had changed their lives—and the life of their son, Fielding—I was astonished. The story was something I'd heard before, but something unlike anything I'd ever heard. It was simultaneously unusual and familiar. And so I knew—if they'd let me—I needed to tell it again.

DOG GONE

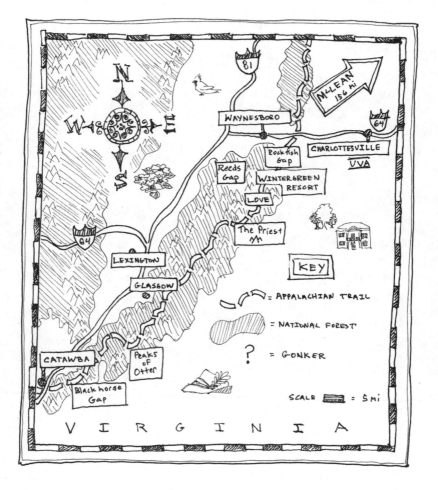

Prologue

A beautiful day on the Eastern Seaboard. Close to sixty-five degrees and sunny—with the scent of autumn in the air and the deciduous trees firing the Appalachians into a blaze of yellow, red, and orange.

William Jefferson Clinton was deep into his tenure as the forty-second president of the United States of America. In the Democratic Republic of Congo, the Great War of Africa—a war that would eventually claim the lives of nearly 5.4 million people—had just begun. In the West Caribbean Sea, atmospheric pressure plummeted, as a mesoscale convective complex—Hurricane Mitch, the second-deadliest Atlantic hurricane of all time—brewed off the coast of Jamaica. The first truly international Windows-based computer virus, the Chernobyl Virus, was crashing hard drives, intercontinentally. France had just beaten Brazil 3–0 in the World Cup Final.

In Kosovo, the U.S. envoy Richard Holbrooke held talks with Slobodan Milošević to resolve the humanitarian crisis, easing tensions between ethnic Albanians and Kosovar Serbs. In Wyoming, four people were charged in the abduction and beating of Matthew Shepard—who lay unconscious in a Laramie hospital, where he would die two days later. In the North Hills neighborhood of Los Angeles, local leaders gathered to dedicate Penny Lane—a county-sponsored apartment complex meant to give housing, education, and counseling to young people with emotional problems. And—on the Appalachian Trail, somewhere on the Blue Ridge Parkway—a golden retriever named Gonker disappeared. He bolted into the trees. He didn't return.

Fielding Corbett Marshall, Gonker's owner—and my brother-in-law—was twenty-eight years old. Fielding and Gonker were, despite their slight biological divergence, best friends. And they were doing a classic American thing—taking a road trip. They'd headed from D.C., where they lived, down to Charlottesville, where Fielding had gone to college. They were revisiting their favorite spots, their old haunts, the houses where Gonker had been a puppy—the couches and kitchens and porches where he'd shed so much of his hair, so many of his fleas, and nearly all of his dignity.

Fielding picked up his human friend Noel, and the three of them drove a couple hours south, to the Jefferson National Forest, so they could enter the Appalachian Trail there and do some hiking. On the trail, Gonker bounded eagerly along, happy to be running in the wilderness. To be loose. To be uncollared. To be doggish. To be *free*.

The forestland in this part of the country is relatively young. It was logged in the 1880s—as the railroads rushed out across America and consumed nearly all of its old-growth forest. Before the railroads, the trees in Appalachia were easily some of the largest in the world. Groves of red spruce, white oak, hemlock, and poplar dotted the hillsides. Individual trees were often one hundred feet tall. Traveling the nearby Kanawha River in 1770, George Washington wrote in his journal: "Just as we came to the hills, we met with a Sycamore of a most extraordinary size, measuring, three feet from the ground, forty-five feet round, lacking two inches; and not fifty yards from it was another, thirty-one feet round."

By the time the Appalachian forests were protected, though, their ecosystem had been transformed. So, unlike the old-growth forests of the Pacific Northwest, which can be so dense in places, the forests where Fielding and Noel and Gonker went for a hike are open. They invite exploration. Especially if you're a dog.

Gonker was running loops on the trail, crashing through the undergrowth with clumsy ardor, chasing squirrels both real and imagined. Fielding kept an eye on him but also paid attention to the sunlight overhead. It was bright and pleasantly cool. The scent of pine hung in the air. Just after noon, the three companions stopped for lunch in a grove of evergreens right off the main path. Fielding was eating raw carrots and bottled water; Noel had a lukewarm cheese-smothered meatball sandwich.

One minute, Gonker was there, standing next to them, sniffing the air, lobbying intently for part of Noel's lunch. And then—he was gone. He darted after something, a swift glimpse of yellow—and then, nothing. Just silence.

Accidents are quick. Bewilderingly quick. It's what survivors of serious car wrecks invariably say: I was amazed by how fast it happened. This is part of why having toddlers—or boisterous, excitable pets—can be so stressful. Disasters lurk there, just off-camera, waiting for the briefest moment to assert themselves.

After fifteen minutes, Fielding began to worry. After an hour, he was seriously concerned. "Gonker!" he started to shout, pacing the same quarter-mile section of trail. "Gonker!" After ninety minutes, Fielding began to panic. Here was the totality of the Appalachian wilderness, confronting him with its vast size. Whereas, before, it had felt manageable, it now felt outsized and daunting. The landscape grew in its immensity.

Fielding and Noel searched and searched. They walked up and down the trail; Fielding yelled until his throat burned. The sun slipped away over the westernmost mountains, twilight rising up around him like the panels of a vise.

"He'll turn up, man," Noel said. "He'll be back, momentarily."

Fielding didn't answer.

"I mean, take your shirt off or something," Noel suggested. "Just toss it down here and he'll smell it and he'll—like—find you. He'll smell you."

Five years out of school, and Noel, who wasn't the most scholarly, was delivering pizza part-time, still living in the same decrepit house he'd lived in during college. But his idea wasn't terrible, all things considered. Fielding pulled his T-shirt off and unceremoniously dropped it on the dirt floor of the forest. He looked at it. The cotton form seemed deflated and empty. He shook his head.

"Haven't we been here before?" he asked. "In this part of the woods?"

"I don't know, man. All the woods are just *trees*, right?"

But Fielding was peering into the distance. Something had caught his attention. There, nearby, a twilit white shape, just off the trail. He squinted. Was it moving?

"Gonker?" he called. And again: "Gonker?"

He took three steps into the undergrowth and then— suddenly—there was only air underneath his boot; he plunged headfirst into a ravine. As he rolled and rolled, everything was a charcoal-colored blur. He came to a stop in a swampy streambed, on his hands and knees, submerged up past his wrists in the viscous black mud.

"Help?" he said quietly, knowing no one else could hear him.

Gonker's story—lost in the wilderness, lost and then sought, sought relentlessly and seemingly beyond the point of hope—is familiar. It's familiar because it's really a story about duty and death, about the way our past shapes our present, and the way we fill our necessary roles most vividly in a crisis. It's a story about responsibility, and illness, and abuse, and generations within a family. It has a megaphone, a map, a mental hospital, a yogi, the governor of Virginia, and—of course—a rare genetic disorder that is both fast-acting and fatal.

And it starts—as you might, or might not, imagine—in a five-star hotel, on the banks of the Ooka River, in downtown Yokohama, Japan.

PART I

The Crucible

Love me, love my dog.
—AESCHYLUS (525–456 B.C.)

1

Here is Virginia Newman Corbett. She will go on to be Fielding Marshall's mother, and Gonker Marshall's grandmother, but right now she is seven years old, a little girl in a bright-red polka-dot dress and bright-red patent-leather shoes. It is 1949. She is in Japan with her parents, and living like a storybook princess.

Here is Lieutenant Colonel William Henry Corbett—Virginia's father, my wife's grandfather—an officer in the United States Army's Special Services Unit, based in Yokohama. Colonel Corbett's job is to approve recreational activities for the soldiers of the American occupation. And so he has to visit—with his family—the hotels and restaurants vying for the business of American GIs. Based on these visits, he recommends certain establishments, and removes others from the lists for officer leave.

Here's how a typical evening went: The car—a limousine—pulled up, bearing Virginia and her parents. The driver opened the door, and the Corbetts stepped out of the vehicle, often onto a red strip of carpet. The staff of the hotel had already assembled in a receiving line; they wore their finest ceremonial dress. The Corbett family then proceeded down that line like royalty—greeting each member of the staff, receiving formal bow after formal bow. Then they went to the central dining room, where they had a many-course meal. There was often a geisha standing near the table who had the sole responsibility of keeping little Virginia happy. Bright silk kimonos, amaranth lipstick, white facial powder, obsidian hair. An intricacy of manners and service.

At the end of these meals, a finger bowl would be put in front of Virginia, a little silver container with warm fragrant water in it—and a white chrysanthemum floating on its surface. She'd dip her fingertips into the bowl, and her geisha would suddenly be there, holding a finely embroidered cloth for her to dry her hands. Virginia thought it was all quite normal and wonderful.

"Eloise at the Plaza," she said, "had nothing on us."

The reality of the economic climate, of course, was this: During the war, Allied forces had firebombed the nation's main industrial centers to rubble. For example, on May 29, 1945, 454 Boeing Superfortress B-29s had hit Yokohama Prefecture, destroying 42 percent of it in just over an hour, killing more than seven thousand people. General Curtis LeMay's 468th Bomb Group had used AN-M76 incendiary bombs filled with PT-1 (Pyrogel) to blanket the city with fire. *Napalm*—blooming in the air and boiling human flesh, nine hundred to a thousand degrees Celsius at the point of ignition.

After LeMay's campaign—and the destruction of

Hiroshima and Nagasaki—Japan's economic infrastructure had to be completely rebuilt. "A better world," General Douglas MacArthur had said during the formal surrender ceremony on board the USS *Missouri*, "shall emerge out of the blood and carnage of the past."

But here is Virginia's mother. Her drinking begins each morning, immediately after breakfast. Or—with increasing frequency—instead of breakfast. The butler makes her a Beefeater gin-and-tonic, the tonic poured over square ice cubes and mixed with a wedge of lime, generously cut, with a bit of sour juice and some pungent, viridescent pulp. Or a Manhattan—Cascade Tennessee whiskey, a dash of Peychaud's bitters, and sweet vermouth in a wide-mouthed glass, a cherry sunk at the bottom like the murky eye of some sightless god. Or a 1929 Château Latour Grand Vin in a bell-shaped glass—a Bordeaux with sweet notes of dark fruit, with a front palette of tobacco, cedar, and plum. Or unfiltered, crystalline vodka—served over crushed ice—if she just needed to do the trick.

Virginia's mother drank all day—slowly, steadily, unceasingly. Whole bottles of sake would disappear, one after another after another. She had no responsibilities in the household; her staff included three full-time live-in maids, a butler, a cook, and a governess.

Adult children of alcoholics will attest to the unmanageability of their parents' behavior, how it is unpredictable and prone to vast swings of temperament. For Virginia, punishment for even the smallest things— leaving an unfolded napkin on the dinner table following a meal, frowning when asked to perform a chore, yawning inappropriately during conversation—was severe.

"Pick a switch," Virginia's mother would say, holding a number of branches out toward her daughter—giving her a choice.

Don't pick the small one, Ginny quickly learned. *The small one hurts the most.* Its tip was voracious; it flayed the skin more easily; it stung and cut like a hungry razor.

A family is fragile. It is destroyed by this kind of violence. The things a child needs—really needs—must be actively, attentively sought. Listening. Patience. Deep time. None of those can be provided by someone who's lost in an alcoholic haze. And so, as she grew—as her needs began to evolve and become more complicated— fissures began to appear in Virginia's porcelain fairy-tale life.

2

By June 1951, the Korean War was in progress, and the U.S. military turned its attention westward from Japan. Personnel on the Japanese archipelago dwindled. And so the army transferred the Corbetts from the splendor of their overseas appointment.

Standing on the dock in Yokohama—saying good-bye to a procession of Japanese officials—the Corbetts received flowers, and cards, and various souvenirs of their time in Japan. The mayor of the city was there, and beside him, on the ground, was a little wicker basket. Virginia kept glancing at it; she swore it moved every time she glanced elsewhere.

The officials presented her mother with a silver brace-let, and a fine silk kimono. They gave her father a box of personalized stationery. And then—the moment that defied all possibility, all expectation—the mayor smiled, bent down to the basket, pulled aside a silk blanket, and took out a small creature, a brown-and-white four-pawed animal that fit in the palm of his hand: an Akita puppy.

He bowed deeply. And then he handed it to Virginia.

"His name is Oji," the mayor said, smiling. "It means 'prince' in Japanese. We hope it will be a reminder of the happy time you spent with us in Japan."

Though Virginia didn't know it at the time, he was a kind of miracle, that inquisitive puppy, the one that put his nose down now and licked persistently at her wrist. In late 1944, the Hirohito government, beset by famine, had ordered all of the nation's nonmilitary dogs euthanized. Dog owners, mad with grief, had turned their beloved pets loose into the wilderness of northern Japan in order to save them. Only eighteen Akitas made it through the war alive. They were survivors, dogs that stood as a symbol of rehabilitation and resilience.

"Virginia—" her mother began, scowling. They couldn't make Virginia return the puppy, could they? And so the little girl didn't give her mother a chance to say anything more. She turned and ran up the gangway. And she hid herself—and Oji—deep within the decks of the ship. No one found her, and she didn't come out until hours after the journey was under way.

The Corbetts returned to the routine of stateside military life, a life that transpired on a series of military bases: El Paso, Texas; Fort Sill, Oklahoma; Colorado Springs, Colorado. The army had located these bases in dusty, rural areas; there were certainly no geishas, no finger bowls, no luxurious ceremonies, no bottomless bottles of fine sake.

Virginia's mother took her disappointment out on her

daughter. "You were so insignificant, Virginia," she'd often say, when even the smallest thing the girl had done displeased her, "that I once left you behind in a crib. Certainly—*certainly*—you'll never amount to anything, my dear."

It was true, Virginia's mother had indeed once left her behind in a crib. It happened during a PCA move—a Permanent Change of Assignment—from one military base to another. Virginia was still a baby. Her mother was drinking heavily that day, and she lost track of her daughter. Left her behind. Left the infant in the crib and drove a load of boxes from one house to the next. Once there, she began to unpack, popped open a beer, and put on a 78. She especially loved the Glenn Miller Orchestra's "Chattanooga Choo Choo," and so she listened to this, and had a few more drinks. She danced her way through the new house, flipping the record again and again, listening to that song, as well as the other side, "I Know Why (And So Do You)." She unpacked a few things, but mostly she didn't. Mostly she just drank. Eventually, she passed out.

When Virginia's mother regained consciousness, it was almost 5:00 p.m.—and quiet. Only then did she realize, *I've left the baby. I've left the baby and I have to retrieve her.* She tried to go on her own, but she couldn't find the car keys. There was no telephone. So she went next door. Here she found another military wife—and explained the situation, as best she could, *laughing* as she did it. She did manage to remember her old address, however, which was lucky. The neighbor rushed off and found Virginia, safe in her crib but dehydrated and weeping, screaming as loud as she could, her lips chapped, her little face red and blotchy.

This story is bad enough on its own. But to imagine that Virginia's mother liked to tell it, for some cruel reason, at cocktail parties with other military couples, while Virginia was in the house, listening to it—this is the truly mysterious thing. The sound of her mother's voice, a syrupy North Carolina drawl, still echoes in Virginia's mind to this day—along with the looping roll of her drunken laughter.

How could she make herself a home in that environment? Endangered, ridiculed, and—above all else—a little girl. In this kind of place, who could be a child's hero? Who would rescue her, and stand by her, in the midst of this vast wilderness of anger and addiction?

The answer, of course, would be Oji. The prince.

3

Oji had grown into a beautiful dog. Stout-backed, brown and white—with big paws and a tail that curled like a question mark.

The Akita is the national dog of Japan—an ancient breed, one that predates the nation's written history. The Akita is famous for its loyalty and bravery. Its renowned fierceness arises, in part, from the fact that it was—for many centuries—bred for dogfights. It was groomed for its size and power. In the mid-nineteenth century, Nakano, an Akita from the foothills of Mount Moriyoshi, in Akita Prefecture, was widely reported as being 35.4 inches tall at the shoulders. His owners would put two children on his back and walk them around the village.

Oji was an Akita Matagi, or Matagi Inu, a bear-hunting dog. Beginning in the Tokugawa era, Japanese hunters would use Akita Matagi to track large game—bears especially, or white-muzzled boars—and trap them in place, until the hunters could arrive to shoot them. Young Virginia sometimes imagined her mother as a bear, and Oji as her tracker. "Mother—cornered in the woods, snarling and snapping, pawing at the dirt with rage. But then Oji, barking and howling, spit flying from his jaws, furious whenever she tried to move." It was her adolescent fantasy.

The most famous Akita, unquestionably, was one named Hachiko. Chuken Hachiko—Faithful Dog Hachiko—belonged to Dr. Hidesaburo Ueno, a professor of agricultural engineering at the University of Tokyo. Starting when he was a puppy in 1924, the Akita would walk with Dr. Ueno to Shibuya Station each morning. Then, each night, he would meet his owner at that same platform. This continued for over a year. Nearly four hundred happy reunions—the dog equally joyous, every time.

But then, on May 21, 1925—a tragedy. Dr. Ueno died, in his office at the university, of a cerebral hemorrhage. That night, Hachiko waited for the train's return; when his owner didn't show, the dog simply went home, to the family residence. And so it would be—every night—for the next ten years. The Akita would walk through the city streets and wait patiently for the evening train. No matter what the weather—fierce heat or swirling snow—he would sit in the place where his owner had once appeared.

Did he dream of the reunion—lying there, resting, waiting for the train that never came? What is an animal's sense of the past? Do their memories work like ours? Do they remember on a reel, the way we can, images from our lost past appearing in our imaginations, unbidden, sudden, almost uncontrollable? After a loss do they dream the way humans do, of the lost individual? Of the beloved? The vanished?

After Hachiko's death in 1935, the station installed bronze footprints—and a plaque—at the point where he'd stood. The statue that commemorates him is the most frequently visited monument in all of Japan. Every year, on March 8—the day the dog died—Shibuya Station holds a solemn memorial, one that is attended by hundreds of dog owners.

For Japan, this story became a story of national importance. In the last photograph of the Akita's dead body, eleven men, two women, and one infant are gathered. All of them avert their eyes from the photographer. They look, instead, at the corpse of the poor animal—stretched on a wooden pallet in front of them. Their hands are clasped together. Their heads are—almost uniformly—bowed in prayer. It is a powerful statement: so many people gathered in prayer for the soul of a single animal.

Like Hachiko, Oji was loyal. Each day, he would wait for Virginia to come home from the military base's elementary school; he'd greet her enthusiastically outside the front door, leaping upward, nipping at her shoulders. Even today—more than six decades later—Virginia Marshall can close her eyes and see him. He surges up into the air, flicks his tail to the left, and seems to laugh—all joy and radiance. Brown and white fur, charged with static electricity, sticks up, uncombed, at every possible angle.

Oji would follow Virginia around the house, as if he sensed her need for protection, going wherever she went, often lingering at the edge of a room or in a doorway, his head resting on his paws, his eyes alert, watchful. But he was also her playmate. One day in January 1953, in the formal dining room, disaster struck.

It is a scene that plays itself out again and again, in almost every country in the world. An eleven-year-old girl and her dog, playing indoors. A tennis ball arcs through the air; a vase plummets to the hardwood floor and shatters into thousands of fragments. The beating Virginia endured as a result of this was unimaginable. At the end of it, her mother staggered away, her own tears mixed with the sweat from the exertion of administering the corporal punishment.

"I need a rest," she said, as her daughter wept and shook on the floor in front of her. "That was just so much work." And then, to her husband: "The dog does not come in the house ever again, you understand? And that's final."

But it was winter in Colorado Springs. Five degrees below zero. Virginia's mother refused to make any provision for Oji outside. Oji spent the night on the front porch, huddled against the seam of the door, trying to get even the smallest amount of heat from the house. In the morning, Virginia made another plea, this time to her father. "Don't bother me," he told her as he left for the day. "Your mother's in charge. It's none of my damn business."

That night, it was supposed to get even colder. Frantic over her dog, and even more frantic over the punishment that she might receive if she countermanded her parents' wishes, Virginia sat in her room, unable to sleep. The house was dark and quiet. She waited an hour, two hours. Finally—when she was sure no one else was awake—Virginia walked to the front door. She sat there for a long time, her palm against the cold wood. And Oji must have smelled her, or sensed her presence somehow, because he began to whimper. She opened the mail slot and whispered: "Oh, Oji. I'm so sorry." And his nose was there, immediately, the tip of it even colder than usual, and his tongue—he was licking the corner of the mail slot, and Virginia's fingertips. She unlocked the door and, as slowly as she could, as quietly, she opened it. The latch creaked. Within seconds he was in her arms, overjoyed, licking her face and smelling her neck, nipping at the collar of her pajamas. She shut the door.

Straining to pick up the seventy-pound dog, Virginia crept back to her bedroom. He seemed to sense that something unusual was happening, because he was quiet; the two of them got through her door and hid under her covers. "There you are, sir," she said, to him, grabbing his wet paws in her hands. "Welcome back." Warm, cocooned by the fabric, Oji's body went limp. Virginia could feel the cold air leaving his fur; she felt his breathing, which had been deep and frantic, normalize. He rested against her, and after a little while they both fell asleep.

And so this became their routine. As soon as the house was quiet, Virginia would sneak down the hallway to the front door. She'd open it and Oji would leap into her arms. They'd go to her room and huddle under the blankets of the bed. In the morning, she was meticulous about cleaning up any fur he might have shed, scrubbing the sheets with a little water where there might be mud. She'd sneak him out the door again before anyone else awoke. It took tremendous self-will and self-discipline to do this without an alarm clock, but Virginia refused to be defeated.

Oji's physicality became a source of comfort for her; she would prop her head on his body and read books to him, by flashlight. "Here we are, Mr. Oji," she'd say. "Here's a good one. *Rabbit Hill*. It's all about an abandoned house—and a family that moves right into it." They'd read a book once, twice, three times—always in a whisper. A particular favorite of the Akita's, Virginia decided, was *The Little White Horse,* a book about an orphan girl—Maria Merryweather—who goes to live with her cousin in his palatial manor house. As they lay there, Virginia confided in Oji, telling him her worries about life, about her family. She'd reminisce about the vanished past—a time that she could never get back to, when she'd felt adored everywhere she went. "Remember when I was a princess, Mr. Oji?" she'd say, holding a little doll in her hand but talking to the dog. "Can you imagine? All the candy you want, all day long?" Virginia would whisper, holding the scruff of his cheeks in her two hands, and the Akita would look at her seriously, considering the question—and sigh.

4

In 1929, in *Civilization and Its Discontents,* Sigmund Freud wrote: "I cannot think of any need in childhood as strong as the need for a father's protection." Virginia's father had long ago abdicated his responsibilities. But, ultimately, her father did one last, tragic thing that broke whatever small bond they may have had. Early one morning in 1953—a morning not long after the family's relocation to Washington, D.C.—Colonel Corbett accidentally backed over Oji while pulling his car out of the driveway.

Virginia came home from school and her companion was gone, shipped off to a veterinarian to dispose of his body.

"I was inconsolable. I couldn't see him, couldn't hold him. But nobody cared. They acted as if it didn't matter."

Here, then, was an absolute violation. Not only had her father failed to protect her, but he'd actively harmed her. He'd killed her only friend—and then he ignored the problem.

"I was so upset," Virginia said, "that I failed the fifth grade."

Virginia wanted only to throw her arms around Oji's rib cage and bury her face in his fur. As she spent more and more nights crying in her room—her homework unfinished on the desk beside her bed—the family acted as if Virginia wasn't even there. "You have to snap out of it, Virginia," her mother told her, her drawl accentuating the slowness of her speech. "The dog's dead, and you can never fix that."

Virginia refused to eat. She'd sit there at dinner, staring down wordlessly at her plate, listening to her parents' voices, following them with only a vague detachment; they were voices from the outside of an aquarium, distant and muffled and mostly incomprehensible. Virginia's teachers had a series of increasingly urgent conferences with Colonel Corbett; since the conferences were in the evening, his wife was never well enough to attend. They recommended rest. And when rest didn't work, they recommended other things. "Have you considered electroconvulsive therapy?" one earnest administrator suggested.

Depression as an acknowledged illness has a relatively short history. Often with depression—especially among the young—symptoms are difficult to distinguish, because the ability to articulate mood is something that comes with age and maturation. For Virginia, in the 1950s, there was no medical infrastructure in place to assist her. The Diagnostic Interview for Children and Adolescents (DICA)—which serves as the benchmark for evaluating kids for mood disorders—was only formulated in the year 2000.

Instead, in the America of 1954, Virginia was taken to a mental institution. On a bright morning in summer, she was awakened by a peremptory shake of her shoulder. Even before she opened her eyes she smelled the gin—that acrid, juniper scent—and tried to burrow more deeply into the pillow.

"Wake up," her mother said. "Out of bed, this instant." And she lifted the girl up and hurried her into her clothes, then ushered her downstairs and out the front door— where a driver was waiting with a car. A long black sedan with a shiny, polished roof, it looked like an insect awaiting its prey.

"Where are we going?" Virginia asked.

Her mother installed her in the back seat. "We're going," she told her thirteen-year-old daughter, "to get you medical help."

The driver started the engine and began—wordlessly— to drive. Virginia chewed her nails, pressing her face against the glass of the window.

"What kind of help?" she asked.

Her mother frowned. "We're taking you for a psychiatric evaluation," she said. "And if it turns out that you are troubled, then we will have you committed."

The car rounded the corner, and there it was—the façade of St. Elizabeths—standing against the horizon like a medieval fortress. The first federally operated mental asylum in the country, St. Elizabeths was established in 1852 by an Act of Congress. When it opened in January 1855, the facility was officially known as the Government

Hospital for the Insane, typically treating the most severe cases—shell-shocked Union soldiers of the Civil War—men driven mad by the violations and brutalities of battle; by hiding behind stacks of corpses under musket fire as lead tore through the dead bodies with a sickening hiss; by combat that often degenerated into muddy brawls with bayonets.

"I'm not sad anymore," Virginia said, looking up at the Gothic hospital towers. "I'm better."

"We'll see what the doctor says about that."

"No, no, Mother. I'll be good—I promise."

But the car kept rolling inexorably forward, and so—on a curve just before the wrought-iron gates—Virginia grabbed the handle and opened the door. She leapt from the moving vehicle.

5

Virginia survived with only cuts and bruises. But the leap did nothing to dissuade her mother, who collected her daughter, dusted her off, and showed up—on time— for the appointment at the hospital. Nurses led Virginia into a large office. The psychiatrist came through a set of double doors, doors that were easily ten feet tall, made of thick burnished oak. He sat on one side of a broad, glass-topped desk. Virginia and her mother sat on the other.

A white laboratory coat. The antiseptic odor of institutional bleach. The leather of the chair; Virginia's palms sweating against it. The window broad and full of light— with birds skittering by—their calls muffled but audible in the silence of the room. The doctor took notes as Virginia's mother detailed—in looping, frantic speech—her daughter's mental problems. He listened gravely. He had a bright-yellow pencil, Virginia remembers, and his glasses were thick bifocals.

"Thank you, Mrs. Corbett," he finally said. "That is all very helpful. But before I can make a diagnosis, I will need to speak with Virginia, alone."

Virginia's mother left the room. The doctor turned his attention to the little girl. He waited a moment, collecting himself.

"Do you know why you're here?" he said.

Virginia didn't answer immediately. But when she finally did, her entire story came out in a torrent: missing her beloved Oji, fearing her mother, being abandoned by her father. The doctor listened impassively to her speech. At first, Virginia was afraid that he would judge her, but then, through tears, she gave up worrying about how she must appear. When she'd finished, the doctor folded his hands on the table. Illumination filled the room; the windows let in light from the outside world.

"Virginia," the doctor said, after a long silence, "do you have any other family nearby? Any grandparents? Is there anyone else you can call?"

"What do you mean?" she asked.

He leaned across the desk and handed her the telephone with its large black rotary dial.

"You need to get out of there," he said. "Now."

Virginia did the only thing she could think of. She called her father's father, her grandfather Munson. Five days later, she went to live with him in Arlington, Virginia. And so—in a way—Oji had saved her.

With Munson Corbett, Virginia would find a home, a home free of the troubles that had so marred her childhood. But one thing continued to haunt her, to stick in her imagination. When she closed her eyes at night—or even during her quieter moments during the day—Virginia still missed her beloved companion. The thing that hurt her most was simple: she'd never had a chance to say goodbye to Oji. And so, forever, this would be Virginia's greatest wish: to redeem her parents' failures, to be responsible for her own family, to take care of them, to be their custodian, their guardian, their ally. No matter what happened, she would give them the chance to get what they most desired.

PART 2

Trait and Trace

I am the family face;
Flesh perishes, I live on,
Projecting trait and trace
Through time to times anon,
And leaping from place to place
Over oblivion.

—THOMAS HARDY, "Heredity"

6

It is 1982. Virginia Corbett is now Virginia Corbett Marshall, but she goes by "Ginny." She is married, and has grown into the person—and the mother—she promised herself she would be. She has two kids—a boy and a girl—a loving husband, and, at this moment, a dead rabbit.

The family has just moved from Wayne, Pennsylvania. And so here is McLean, their new home: a wealthy suburb of Washington, D.C.—a suburb where the houses are far apart and set on landscaped, rolling lawns. Down the street from the Marshall residence is the home of Dick Cheney—the United States congressman from Wyoming—who will soon become the nation's seventeenth secretary of defense and, eventually, vice-president under George W. Bush. Every driveway has a Mercedes or a Cadillac. One property, just a few lots away, has a custom-built tennis court in its backyard.

Here is Peyton, the inconsolable owner of the dead rabbit. She is ten years old, and wearing orthodontic headgear. She is painfully thin, and barefoot. She sobs, at intervals, into the oversized sleeve of her purple velour sweatshirt.

Here is Fielding, the son, twelve years old, acting as if he is bored out of his mind. He has, but only after repeated demands, surrendered his Sony Walkman. He lags behind the family, slightly. In a few minutes—when his sister begins to cry in earnest—he will edge forward and sheepishly hold her hand.

Ginny has carefully sealed the rabbit in a Ziploc bag, smoothing its ears flat against its body, tucking its little paws under its torso—all the while crying herself. She has taken that Ziploc bag and nestled it in a tissue-paper-lined shoe box.

Here are Godfrey and Thistle, the family dogs—watching with attentiveness the exact location of the burial.

Here is John—Ginny's husband—Fielding and Peyton's father. He has a shovel. "Dearly beloved," he says. His voice cracks with inappropriate amusement.

"Johnny," Ginny scolds.

"Sorry, sorry," he says. He clears his throat. He begins again. "Dearly beloved, we are gathered here today to remember . . ." He looks at Peyton.

"Thumper Dumper," Peyton says.

"Right," he says. "She was a high-strung rabbit. She didn't like to be held or touched. She was a biter and a scratcher."

Ginny clears her throat.

"But we loved her," John says quickly.

"And now the dogs will eat her," says Fielding.

"Amen," John says.

Ginny turns to hold her weeping daughter. The shovel goes into the earth. The box goes into the dirt. In many ways, it is a grand coffin. And so the Marshalls give Thumper Dumper an elaborate—even somewhat extravagant—farewell.

Ginny and John had met in November 1963, on the day after the assassination of President Kennedy. On the evening of November 23, Ginny had attended a house party in the city. The hosts—having planned their occasion months before—had decided to go ahead with the event, figuring people would welcome a chance to get together and share their grief. Like most everyone else at the event, Ginny had felt quiet and subdued.

After an hour or so, however, she'd come around the corner into the kitchen and found a little knot of people. In the center, there he was—an enthusiastic, lean, bushy-eyebrowed young man, holding a highball glass in one hand and gesturing with the other. He was in the middle of a story, his eyes narrow with amusement, his head tilted back slightly, as if he could almost taste the joy of the unfolding narrative.

"As Boy Scouts we all did our own cooking, you understand," he was saying. He noticed Virginia and motioned for her to join the circle. "We'd go to the Kreidersville store and buy lots of Wonder Bread, and a dozen eggs, and a big jug of milk. We'd make French toast for twenty boys. The griddle was red-hot—you know, heated on the fire. And so we'd soak a piece of Wonder Bread— get it good and wet—and then we'd set the soggy milk ball down on the griddle and it would sear. The French toast would develop this lovely black crust on it, which of course would hold it all together. And so we'd slip the spatula under it and flick it into the air and onto a plate and hand it to a hungry twelve-year-old. He'd look at it with big eyes. And of course he knew, that's all he's getting to eat. So he'd pour lots of King Syrup on it and—down it went." He trailed off, laughing along with everyone else. "Everybody was starving all the time."

"Sounds like you're a professional chef," Ginny said.

The young man smiled. "I was just sharing some stories from my time with Dan Tyrell, scout leader of Troop 100 of the Boy Scouts of America." He looked toward her, his eyes bright. "I'm John Marshall," he said. "Pleased to meet you."

"Ginny Corbett," Virginia said, and smiled, and shook his hand.

After the party, Ginny ended up in a car with John, driving to Georgetown with two other couples, to the Bayou—a bluegrass bar that was having its weekly talent night. Aspiring country-and-western singers would drive in from the Chesapeake region and perform there, hoping this was the first step on the road to stardom. There had been some question whether they'd have the show that night, given the circumstances. But when Virginia had called to double-check, the hostess had answered on the first ring.

"Hell, yeah," the woman had said. "We'll be here—singin' and drinkin' and cryin'."

Of all that night's performers, Virginia thought that one young man was especially talented. He'd dedicated his performance to the fallen president. But when the judges announced the winners—one champion and two runners-up, he wasn't among them. The crowd booed. A bottle shattered on the wooden floor.

Ginny would often keep a Christmas ornament in her hair, a festive gesture, an accent, a conversation piece. Often, people would ask her about it, and if it was an antique it could bridge to a discussion of the rituals of Christmas in general, or the history of ornamentation. On that night, she went over to the singer. He was packing up his guitar, an egg-yellow Fender Champ lap steel, whose polished wooden finish shone even under the dim lights of the bar.

"You were terrific," she told him, without introduction. "It's a crime you didn't win."

"Thank you, ma'am," he said.

"No," Ginny insisted. Tears came into her eyes. "I just can't believe it. You were the best." And then she took the ornament—a bright silver globe with red piping—and handed it to him.

He frowned. "I'm not certain where I'd put this, ma'am," he said.

"Well," Ginny said, "did you drive here?"

"Yes, ma'am. From my farm out near Warrenton."

"Then you can put it in your glove box," she said, "and keep it there for luck. Problem solved?"

The man looked from her to the little glass globe, then back to her insistent, unblinking face. He smiled. "Problem solved, ma'am," he said.

John watched from their table. Later, he would tell her, "That's the moment I fell in love with you."

Together with John, Ginny would build a family. She would seek to fix the things that had broken so long ago in her life, applying that indomitable force of will to the problem of raising children. No matter what the issue, Ginny would always persist; she would seek to interrupt the chaos and disorder and unfairness of living. If her parents hadn't been present for her, she would always be present for her kids. If her own toys had been meager and disorganized, she would provide Fielding and Peyton with an array of labeled, compartmentalized playthings. If she'd missed out on a stable and structured childhood, she would provide one for the next generation.

There were rules—lots of rules. A sit-down family dinner. No hats at the dinner table. Clean your plate. Sit with one hand in your lap, atop your napkin. Once a week, participate in a formal meal in the dining room, so that you will be comfortable in any kind of social gathering. Sparkle your personality. One hour of educational television per day. No outdoor shoes indoors. Don't slam the front door. Don't leave the front door open. No kicking, biting, punching, slapping, or horseplay of any kind. No drawing on the wall. Do not pet strange animals.

This last rule, especially, was difficult to enforce. Peyton and Fielding brought home pet after pet. There were crawfish, caught in the stream behind the house and transported in buckets of mud. There was a frog—a surprise tenant of the downstairs bathroom, installed ceremoniously in the sink, with scraps of grass and rocks, for habitat. There was a baby squirrel, which somehow crawled up Peyton's leg at a birthday party. Of course there were two kittens, found in an alley. There was a baby mouse named Timothy.

Timothy's case was particularly dire. A handsome white mouse with little black eyes, he was a rescue of sorts, purchased from a pet store that had stocked him as snake food. He lived in a sawdust-floored tank in the mudroom. After a long life for a mouse—nearly two happy years at the Marshall residence—he developed a large, purulent tumor on the back of his neck.

"What is that?" Fielding asked Peyton. "It looks like he's growing a second head."

And so, one Saturday, Virginia, John, Peyton, and Fielding all piled into the car and took the mouse to the veterinarian. The vet looked very seriously at Timothy, examining him with a magnifying glass. His expression was somber.

"It could be benign," he said finally. "But we'll have to remove it."

"Great," John said. "And how much does that cost?"

"I'm not completely certain," the vet said, frowning. "But you're looking at, probably around one hundred dollars—"

"A hundred dollars!" John exclaimed. "I bought a *car* for a hundred dollars in 1958."

"—and fifty dollars for a privacy curtain."

"Privacy?" John said. "For a mouse?"

"It's so they can't see the operation."

"I *want* him to see the operation," John said. "We're spending a hundred dollars to save the mouse's life."

The mouse came home with recovery instructions, mimeographed in purplish-black ink. Once a week he was to have a sulfur bath in the kitchen sink. The sulfur would inhibit the regrowth of the tumor, the veterinarian assured them. "There's no telling how long he might live," he said.

For the next year, every Sunday night, Ginny filled the sink with bright-yellow sulfured water. It smelled like rotten eggs. Peyton or Fielding would then take the mouse from its cage and carry it over to Ginny. The ability of mice to learn from experience cannot be questioned— Timothy would clutch in fear to the children's arms, squirming to avoid his medical treatment—so Ginny had to take over the job. Her wrists were covered in long thin scratches all that year—the work of one mouse, and its fearful, desperate claws.

7

The one time Peyton and Fielding met their grandmother, she was wearing a red-and-black sequined gown, and she lay in bed—at one in the afternoon—fully made up, her gray hair perfectly curled. It was 1986, on a family vacation. Ginny had decided, after much anguish, that her children should, at least once, stand face-to-face with their grandmother. The Marshalls had rented a Winnebago and were headed for the coast of Florida. All that first day, John and Ginny drove in tense silence. They were normally at their most vocal on family road trips—with John concocting songs about the Open Road, and Ginny structuring activities around the sights of the trip: collecting the names of the towns they passed on the highway, playing the alphabet game with the license plates of other cars. But not this time.

When John and Ginny got married, they'd reserved the chapel at Arlington National Cemetery, a common loca-

tion for weddings—especially within military families.
It was November 27, 1965. Immediately before the
ceremony—seeing Ginny begin to tear up—the organist
leaned close to her. "No time for crying," he said. "We're
on a tight schedule. Ten couples today." There were ceremonies every hour, on the hour. Ginny had invited her
entire family. Only two of them came: Munson and,
grudgingly, her father.

Ginny had always dreamed of a wedding party in
morning dress—the long-tailed, single-breasted coat for
the men, together with striped trousers, and suspenders.
But her father had objected—on the day of the wedding.
He'd arrived in the clothes she asked for, but brought his
army uniform with him, and now he demanded that she
wait for him to go and change his clothes.

"I'll look best wearing these," he said, pointing to his
uniform. "I'll look appropriate, at least."

"It's my marriage," Ginny said, "not yours."

The organist began to play Henry Purcell's "Trumpet
Voluntary." Colonel Corbett looked at his daughter. He
frowned. And then he turned and took the first step down
the aisle—nearly making her stumble, he pulled her along
so violently.

"I feel like a jackass in this," he said over his shoulder.

Of course, her mother had not shown up. Years later,
Ginny learned that her mother had, in fact, been there.
She'd taken a taxi to the chapel and stayed in the taxi
throughout the ceremony, off to one side of the entrance,
with the meter running. She'd watched her daughter

emerge, a married woman. And then, without saying anything, she'd driven away.

Now, however, Ginny was driving toward her. On the morning of the trip's second day, the Marshalls found themselves on an unmarked dirt road not far from Seaboard, North Carolina. There were a few houses; the lots were demarcated by rusted chain-link fencing. But mostly this was farmland, only some of which had been cultivated; much of it lay fallow.

When they arrived, no one greeted them. The door was hanging open. "Hello?" Ginny called, stepping into the interior of the house. "Hello?"

And yet she knew where to find her. Instinctively, she knew. She headed up the stairs and to the main bedroom. And there her mother was, awaiting her daughter and her daughter's family, a bottle of red wine on the bedside table.

"Aha," Ginny said, stepping through the doorway. "There you are."

Her mother smiled, eyes glassy.

"How lovely that you all could join us today," she said.

Ginny shook her head and sighed. "Peyton, Fielding—this is Louise Anne Slocumb, my mother."

In those words—*my mother*—there was something crucial. Ginny didn't introduce her as "your grandmother." It was almost as if she didn't want the relationship to touch her children; she didn't want them to have any kind of bond with this woman. If humanity's luminous genetic code can be thought of as a polychromatic brush—a fibrous cable like the cable of a bridge—then Ginny can be imagined as unraveling it, or trying to unravel it, seizing one of the colors and extracting it, or trying to extract it.

Peyton stared. Mostly, she was shocked to hear the full name, which she'd never heard before. *Louise Anne Slocumb*. It felt like a fist.

Fielding rallied. He dipped his head. "Nice to meet you," he said—his voice simulating the speech of a robot.

Ginny was silent. Her mother didn't reply.

One beat. Two beats. Three.

"Louise," John finally said, "why don't we just go downstairs and give you a little time to collect yourself?"

The neighbors had a trampoline, something the kids had spotted on the way in. "Let's get out of here," Fielding whispered to Peyton, and the two of them rushed downstairs and back out the front door, never to cross that threshold again. It would also be the last time Ginny saw her mother alive.

Later, long after their visit, a night in September, Ginny and John came home from dinner in the city. They returned to a dark house, except for the kitchen with its yellowish lightbulbs, its buttery nighttime glow. The dishwasher was running. The babysitter—eighteen years old, barely older than Fielding and Peyton—was reading *The Clan of the Cave Bear* and chewing voraciously on fruit-scented bubble gum.

Ginny paid her, handing over a five-dollar bill.

"The kids didn't really eat," the girl said as she put on her coat. "The pizza's in the fridge, and—oh—your father called to say that your mom died."

The funeral—attended by almost no one—would be on a sunny, beautiful day. And as her mother's body entered the earth, a single bird called out, over and over again, the same cry—the same note, plangent, persistent.

And Ginny suddenly thought, without willing it: *I forgive you.*

8

Growing up in Washington, D.C., in the 1980s: The punk subculture was roiling the suburbs. Nuclear war was a virtual certainty. Peyton says: "I figured that *when* the war came I'd just go out and sit on the lawn. Better to be burnt up than to hang on and survive in a nuclear winter."

Ginny wanted—desperately wanted—her children to participate in family rituals. The rules of the house were significant—and somehow always growing. And as Peyton and Fielding became teenagers, they cared about these requirements less and less. They understood their mother's need for order, but they didn't pause—not really—to speculate about its roots. To have compassion for it.

"We will all sit together at the table for a meal," Ginny would say, "and each share something noteworthy from our day." Or, when no one appeared: "Please, can we all sit down and speak to each other in a civil manner—engaging in a polite conversation." Or: "It's dinnertime. Fielding, Peyton, please come downstairs."

The house had an intercom. Fielding recorded Virginia speaking into the system. He'd wait for her to finish and then push down the talk button himself—playing her voice back throughout the house in a scratchy, reverberating echo.

"Mom," he'd eventually say, "you're just saying the same thing over and over and over—that's so weird."

"You should really have that checked, Mom," Peyton would add, getting on her intercom.

"Yeah," Fielding would say, "we're worried about you."

"You should rest, Mom," Peyton would say. "Is it dinnertime?"

Of course, what Fielding and Peyton didn't see—what they could never imagine—was their mother weeping in the kitchen after they'd both gone to bed. She was working so hard, trying so hard to make their childhood magical. No—ideal, an ideal childhood. And surely their behavior was evidence of her failure. She could not control them; they wouldn't come to dinner when she called; they wouldn't behave properly anywhere they needed to; she could not get close enough to make them understand.

There was, of course, the matter of Benson, the family's bichon frise. The Marshalls had adopted Benson from the Humane Society of Fairfax County on Chain Bridge Road; his previous owners, the Humane Society warned them, had found his barking unbearable. And it was. Peyton, Fielding, John—and even Ginny—found themselves hollering, *"Benson! Quiet!"* at all hours of the day and night.

Benson barked at cars on the street outside, or squirrels in the trees, or birds in the birdfeeder, or joggers, or mailmen, or utility-company personnel. He would often sneak into a room—a room, for example, where Peyton was studying—and wait until his presence was almost certainly forgotten, and then leap up suddenly, issuing his loudest, fiercest howl. He barked at changes in the weather.

Home alone one afternoon, just after school, Fielding and Peyton stumbled on an explanation: Benson was bored. *This* was the root of his overactive barking. Peyton herself, often bored as well, really enjoyed the process of dyeing her hair. And hair was a lot like fur, wasn't it? So why *not* augment Benson's plain white coat with something a little less staid? A little more festive? More colorful.

"What do you think, Fields?" Peyton asked Fielding one night, after they'd finished their homework and shown it to their mother. "Should we dye the dog?"

"Do you mean," Fielding said, "which color should we pick?"

They invited Benson into the bathroom with a Milk Bone. That part was easy. Then they put on raingear to protect themselves from the squirming, soon-to-be-colored animal. They fed him more Milk Bones. They applied the food coloring. Peyton started with just the peripheries—some blue on the tips of the ears, some red on the end of his tail, some green on the tops of his paws. Accents, really. And one or two squares—*nothing*

too bold—on his body. And then a few stripes. Kind of a
Mohawk thing. He looked quite fetching, Peyton thought.
He was a punk-rock dog now.

Ginny came through the door, tired and thinking
about dinner, carrying her pocketbook and a stack of
paperwork in an overstuffed binder. The kids heard the
whir of the motor for the automatic garage-door opener.
They scurried upstairs. They heard the key in the lock.
The lock turned. The door opened. Benson ran, yelping,
to greet Virginia.

There was a moment of silence. Then, in a voice that
was both a declaration and a wail: "Oh no! Oh no! What
have you done? How could you? What—*what* have you
done?" Footsteps to the stairs. "Fielding! Peyton!" Footsteps back toward the door. "Oh God—he looks like a
rainbow."

The teenagers collapsed into each other, a writh-
ing, giggling pile. *Aha,* they thought. *Amazing.* Because
this—this was power. It was currency. A shared currency
of parental frustration. A joyous collaboration. A mad-
ness, of sorts. A fever.

Later that night, whispering in Peyton's room, Fielding said: "Can you imagine them walking a purple dog
around the neighborhood? I mean—all purple. Solid
purple."

"Semi-permanent?" Peyton said.

"Sure," Fielding said. "It's camouflage."

"For what?" she said.

Fielding paused. "For anything purple?" he said, and for some reason this made the two of them break into uncontrollable laughter.

That week, Peyton procured an extra tub of Ultra Violet at Commander Salamander. One Wednesday night—with Ginny and John safely in the basement, watching a movie—Fielding and Peyton sprang into action. They rushed Benson into the garage and showed him the tub of hair dye. As for the dog, he seemed to love it: *who knew that Benson was such a fan of Manic Panic?* To Benson, it was just an elaborate and protracted spell of petting; he was being praised and—*yes, admittedly*—transformed somewhat. But it was worth it, right? For the petting? And the Milk Bones. More and more and more Milk Bones. What a terrific night! What a great idea! He rushed downstairs and leapt—bright purple and slightly wet—into Ginny's lap. Her shriek was audible on all levels of the house.

Later—forced back into the garage to clean Benson off—Fielding decided that, really, it would be much more efficient to shave him. And so he and Peyton set about the task, using an old set of electric clippers whose buzzing noise spooked Benson a bit. He whined, but they kept feeding him dog biscuits, and they were able to get almost all of him shaved before Ginny heard the noise of the clippers. She opened the door—her curiosity switching to alarm.

"No!" she yelled, rushing over and reaching for the plug. "What were you thinking?"

And so, for the next four weeks—as Fielding had predicted—Virginia walked her mostly shaved, still faintly purple dog around the neighborhood. But Fielding had underestimated his mother's resourcefulness. In her closet, she had a small woolen sweater—one that was the perfect size for a bichon. Benson looked mostly normal— except, of course, for his single purple leg.

9

March 1991. Latvia voted for its own independence—seceding from the Soviet Union and ending nearly five decades of foreign occupation of Latvian soil. United Airlines Flight 585 crashed in Colorado Springs—its rudder power control unit suddenly destabilized, the plane plummeting eighty-five hundred feet in nine seconds and crashing into Widefield Park, killing twenty-five passengers and crew, its impact crater fifteen feet deep and thirty-four feet wide. Los Angeles police pulled over and severely beat Rodney King—unaware that the beating was being videotaped. Exxon agreed to pay one billion dollars in fines for the cleanup of the *Exxon Valdez* disaster. Albania held its first democratic election in fifty years. The UN Security Council voted to lift the food embargo on Iraq. And Fielding Marshall—his red hair an unruly tangle, his face awash with freckles from spending too much time in the sun—was a junior at the University of Virginia in Charlottesville.

Charlottesville was only a three-hour drive from

McLean, but it was quite different from suburban Washington. It was a smaller town, one dominated by the events of university life, by its seasonal rhythms and crowds of undergrads roaming in search of cheap food, clothes, records, and—most importantly—beer.

By now, Fielding had lost his co-conspirator; Peyton had moved across the country to attend Reed College, in Portland, Oregon. Fielding was lonelier, sure, but he was also busy—far too busy, for example, to shower. He wore Teva sandals over thick wool socks. He ate Snickers bars for breakfast. It was four years before the death of Jerry Garcia, but bootleg Grateful Dead tapes littered the dirty floor of Fielding's Nissan 300ZX. He liked to drive the car up to the Appalachian foothills and park on the side of the road. He'd pop in a cassette and sing along to "Sugar Magnolia," as loud as he could, stoned.

Fielding met her at a party. Thin, beautiful, with sleek brown hair and a loose-fitting linen peasant blouse— bright red with silver embroidery around the collar— she was standing by herself, sipping a glass of sparkling water. She was someone he sort of knew—the girlfriend of a friend's friend, a few degrees of separation. She introduced herself as Rebecca. Rebecca Hillsdale. She'd just come from yoga. As they talked, Fielding revealed that he was also a yoga practitioner.

"I'm deeply devoted," he told her.

"Really?" Rebecca said.

"Of course," Fielding said. "I mean—I am now." He smiled. She smiled back.

He quickly found out the rest of the story. The boy-friend—the friend of a friend—had left town. And so Fielding volunteered to accompany Rebecca to a few yoga classes. One evening, they went back to her apartment. They had a few glasses of wine. He spent the night.

In the morning, in bed, Rebecca lay beside him. "I have something to tell you," she said. She moved her body against his, nuzzling underneath his unshaven chin. She paused. He waited there, listening to the sound of his own breath rising and falling, an even metronome. "One of the classes I'm taking," she said, "it's a prenatal class."

A pause. Another heartbeat.

"Okay," Fielding said. His voice was level.

"Okay, what?" she said. And there was a touch of some unruly emotion in her voice, something that—perhaps—Fielding should have noticed. But Rebecca thought he hadn't understood. "I'm going to have a baby," she said.

He paused. "That's cool," he said. "Lots of people have babies."

She frowned. "But do lots of them wake up with you on a Saturday morning?"

Fielding looked her in the eyes. "Not that many," he said. And he glanced down at her bare shoulder, almost luminescent in the dim light of the morning. The idea of how vulnerable she was—the very fact that she was sheltering another human life inside of her—was powerful to Fielding.

"What does it feel like?" he asked.

"A countdown," Rebecca said. "I don't completely believe it myself."

"I'm glad you're here, then."

"Me, too," she said.

"Do you want it to be a boy or a girl?"

"I want it to be a surprise," she said.

And so Fielding cupped his hands over Rebecca's belly. Why couldn't he be a protector? he thought. Maybe this was exactly what he needed. Maybe this would help him become the person—in his heart—he longed to be. After all, why couldn't he fill that role? He was resourceful, intelligent, fun to be with. He imagined himself forward into time: Playing catch with his daughter at the park. Walking with her to the bus stop every morning. Teaching her about Roman history—a subject that, thanks to John, he happened to know quite a lot about. His mind flooded with gauzy, hopeful images. Why couldn't he be a role model? Why couldn't he be a surrogate dad?

10

Hatha is a Sanskrit word meaning "the act of pillage or plundering," or "obstinacy," or "forcefulness," or, interestingly, "slaughter." And though some argue that the word "yoga" comes from the word for "magical art," or "union of the individual soul with the universal soul," there is just as much evidence to support its being a derivation of the word for "yoke." Whatever the case, there is no doubt that it was once intended, at least in part, to calm the minds of soldiers—and strengthen their bodies— before they went into battle.

Rebecca loved the emptiness of the practice, especially at a time when she herself was filling with another life. Fielding, in turn, loved Rebecca.

"I've heard," she taught him, "that Shiva himself first explained the postures to the goddess Parvati. He thought they were alone on an island when he was explaining them, but a fish overheard the whole thing, and later became the great yogi Matsyendranath."

The narrative was fascinating, and in 1991 it felt like they were discovering it on their own. There was only one yoga studio in Charlottesville: a converted barn where an old woman who'd once studied with Indra Devi held daily classes. Fielding and Rebecca were there every day, sometimes staying for a double class. And they were astounded by the intimacy of partner yoga. Fielding would lift Rebecca off the ground and into the air, her hands clasping his shoulders, his feet supporting her weight. There she was, suspended above him, looking directly into his eyes.

Tenzin Wangyal Rinpoche was just setting up the Ligmincha Institute outside of town. Rinpoche was an advocate of lucid dreaming; he taught Tibetan movement practices and was a practitioner of the Dzogchen meditative tradition. Fielding found himself driving out to the compound with Rebecca and having long talks with the monks about the discipline of self-denial and the attainment of yogic bliss—a state of luminous and pure mind, where the body's desires have been dissolved. The ideas were shocking and exciting; he and Rebecca had long arguments about the difference between development (*kye*), perfection (*dzog*), and great perfection (*dzogchen*). Afterward, he'd have hallucinatory dreams about gods talking to fish, and strange yoga classes under the surface of the ocean.

Despite—or perhaps because of—this, Fielding learned quickly. In a few months he petitioned the university's Student Activities Board to allow him to teach yoga classes on campus. They approved the petition, and so he became the first yoga instructor in the state of Vir-

ginia's university system. He battled with the Christian
Student Ministries, who saw his practice as a religious
cult. They'd hand out fliers before his classes: "YOGA,"
the fliers read. "JUST EXERCISE? OR A HINDU CULT?"

"I'm so much more interesting than I thought I was,"
he told Rebecca, reading to her from a leaflet.

"Just wait until you tell them about lucid dreaming,"
she said.

Soon they moved in together, in order to have everything
settled when the baby arrived. Rebecca took up residence
in his downtown apartment, filling it with her stuff—her
furniture and clothes and records and books and kitchen-
ware and unusual Indian spices, the jars of turmeric and
cardamom and cumin seed. And then, two months later,
Ginny and John drove down to Charlottesville to go out
to dinner with them.

On the road from Washington, D.C.—making the
beautiful drive through the Shenandoah Valley—Ginny
practiced what she was going to say, trying to become
more gracious, to strengthen a feeling that she wished she
had. "I'm sure she's a very nice girl," she told John. "I'm
sure they'll be very happy together."

"What makes you so sure?" he said.

"I'm sure they'll be very happy together," Ginny
repeated, with a renewed conviction. "It's whatever they
want—not what we want, John."

"But I have an opinion," John said.

"That's not relevant, dear," Ginny said. "Just drive."

Rebecca was deeply pregnant—nearly thirty-eight weeks. At dessert, when she left to go the restroom, Ginny leaned in and whispered to her son, "Have you considered this decision carefully, Fields?"

"Every day, Mom," Fielding said. "Every minute, every hour."

"Seriously," Virginia said, "this isn't something to rush into. Some more reflection might be useful. Maybe you might pray about it? Why not? That's certainly an option, isn't it?"

"Religion," Fielding said, "is the opiate of the masses."

"Glad to see you're doing your homework, son," John said, as Rebecca returned to the table.

You have to consider that Fielding was really just a kid. He was a young man who'd yet to work a full-time job, yet to support himself in the world. Of course he was unprepared. He was unprepared for all of it—for sharing his life with another person, for the compromises and stresses of life on life's terms. He was most unprepared, perhaps, for one basic experience: the stress of the delivery. He was unprepared for the pacing in the waiting room, as the minutes became hours; the buzz of the voices on the television, somehow just beyond understanding, filling the air with a kind of sad noise. And he was certainly unprepared for the doctor's entering the waiting room, his face gaunt and serious.

"She's asked us to tell you that there's been a complication."

Fielding found himself moving through a series of fluorescent-lit hallways, following the physician. He found Rebecca in the hospital bed, barely able to move, even more pale—drained of blood by the difficult labor. The baby was down the hall, cocooned in glass, intubated, impossibly small, and surrounded by a galaxy of medical equipment. An infant in the NICU is a half-formed thing. Born—but not quite. A tiny creature, unable to live on its own, its heart built incorrectly, congenitally broken.

But in that first moment—that moment when he was still struggling to understand what had happened—Fielding nonetheless had to be there for Rebecca, to support her however he could. She looked at him as he came up to the bed and stood beside her. "Her fingers," she said. Rebecca's cheeks were red and puffy from crying. "They were so tiny."

"It's not so bad," Fielding said, his voice breaking. "It could be worse."

"How? How exactly, Fields, could it be worse?"

But he didn't have an answer.

The baby girl died within months—in the midst of an operation to repair her heart. She lived just long enough for Fielding to fall deeply in love with her—for him to feel the need to protect and save her. And so, after her death, here it came: an oceanic wave of sorrow.

Rebecca blamed Fielding for all of it; she was looking for anyone to blame. They fought and fought. About what? What do people fight about when they can't access the real thing that they're fighting about? People who are simply fighting about the cruelty of fate and chance and genetic circumstance? Nothing in particular—or, everything. The proper way to do a certain pose; the stack of books splayed on the coffee table; the dinner plans forgotten; plans for the next week, the next month, the next year. Rebecca was also struggling with jealousy; whenever Fielding even talked with another woman at a party, she felt the tenuous nature of her hold on him. She also felt the wounding of her own body, which had been stretched and remade—for a future that hadn't turned out to be viable. It was an unfulfilled promise.

"Do you love me?" she asked him again and again, in almost any circumstance, any location.

"Of course I love you."

"It's my fault, though?"

"Of course it's not your fault."

"But do you love me?"

"I already told you. I've told you a hundred times. Come on."

"Why are you yelling?"

"I'm not yelling."

The fights were long and intricate and intense. And then, one afternoon, in December 1991, Fielding came home from work and the apartment was empty. She'd packed everything in five hours. All her possessions, her clothes, her books, her rudimentary furniture. She'd crammed it into her car and disappeared—a carefully

orchestrated departure. As he walked around the suddenly empty apartment, he put his hand on the coffee
table where she'd just that morning rested her oversized
coffee mug. He touched the space where it had left a ring
on the glass.

"No," he said aloud. He turned back toward the door.
"No," he said again.

The scent of Rebecca still lingered in the air. He realized that, coming into the empty apartment, he'd forgotten to shut the door. Cold air rushed in now, making him
shiver and shake. Fielding sat down on the dusty floor,
put his head in his hands, and then—surprising even
himself—began to cry.

He would remember that night always, of course: the
empty apartment, the things he didn't even expect to miss,
such as bottles of prenatal vitamins, stacks and stacks of
diapers, boxes of tiny clothes, the breast-feeding pillow.
He sat in the middle of the living-room floor and tried
to summon the smallest amount of serenity—anything
at all—but he couldn't find it. His breath, usually a tool
to lead him toward meditation, was pinched and unruly;
he couldn't calm down his thudding heart. But there was
also a feeling deeper inside of his body—an unusual,
gnawing ache, deep within his abdomen, just beneath
his stomach. Like his mother before him, Fielding hadn't
had the chance to say goodbye. But also, as for her, a dog
would start the process of saving his life.

PART 3

The Puppy

Why can't you get over it?
I don't know, I don't know.
Why don't you get over it?
I don't know, I don't know.
Why won't you get over it?
I don't know, I don't know.
Why can't you get over it?
I don't know, I don't know.
—THE THIRD SEX, "Mombies"

11

It was raining heavily on the night when Fielding walked out of the Charlottesville Albemarle SPCA—holding an eight-week-old golden retriever mix of unknown origins. Lacking an umbrella, Fielding sheltered the little dog underneath his windbreaker. Heat lightning flickered in the thunderous sky.

Have you ever held a puppy in your hands? He doesn't often stay in your hands unless you try to keep him there—which isn't terribly difficult, after all. But it does take some concentration. If you don't concentrate, he will inevitably wiggle out of your grasp and begin to climb your arm. And then, perhaps, climb onto your chest, and your shoulders, and your head. A puppy is ambitious.

Had Fielding looked closely, he might have seen some of the American Kennel Club's characteristics of the golden retriever breed: the dense, water-repellent coat; the broad skull, slightly arched laterally, but without prominent occipital bones; the muzzle straight in profile; the eyes friendly and intelligent in expression, medium-large with dark, close-fitting rims. Originally bred in nineteenth-

century England by the first baron of Tweedmouth—
Dudley Marjoribanks—golden retrievers are one of the
most thoroughly genetically matching breeds: they share
99.9 percent of each other's DNA. And though the puppy
was a mutt, there was clearly a golden in his very recent
past.

Fielding, however, didn't notice any of this. Instead,
he said, "What's up, pup?" and slid behind the steering wheel, lifting the little guy up into the air. Fielding's
plan—the result of several months of loneliness—was to
find a creature, a dog in need of a home, and provide that
shelter. Beyond that, there wasn't really much to it.

On that first night, he'd simply intended to hold the
puppy in his lap and drive home with him cradled close
to his body. But within seconds the puppy began to pee, a
glistening, translucent stream of warm urine that arched
through the air and soaked Fielding's shirt and pants and
the driver's seat of his Nissan.

"Fuck!" he said, and the puppy interpreted this as a
playful bark. He wiggled free of Fielding's hands and
then, with a squeal of joy, leapt onto the passenger seat.
Then he yipped. Fielding was dripping wet and distracted,
and so he didn't at first see the puppy lunging for the gear-
shift and attaching himself to the knob of it, like a leech
latching on to an elbow.

"Hey! Down!" But the dog had begun to chew on the
little plastic knob. "Watch out! That's part of the car!"

Somehow, Fielding had managed to press down on the
clutch—and now the Nissan was in reverse. The puppy

had shifted them into reverse gear, and they were rolling slowly backward out of their parking space. Fielding hit the brakes—and stopped immediately before entering the lane of traffic.

Cars flashed by, going forty miles an hour on the arterial.

In their first moments together, the little guy had nearly killed them both.

12

In pictures from those months in early 1992, more often than not Fielding is barefoot, and only rarely is he wearing anything that isn't tie-dyed. Though he wasn't a member of a Grateful Dead cover band, he had taught himself many of their songs on the guitar. He moved, with a few of his friends (some of whom *were* in a Grateful Dead cover band), into a house in the woods outside of town. This particular house could, generously, be called a "cabin."

"It was a shack," Ginny says. "There was a sofa on the porch, and when you sat down, the dust billowed up over you in a cloud. There was a refrigerator in the front yard. I think they kept beer in it."

Ramshackle. Someone told Fielding that the house had been built—in a rush—by bootleggers in the 1920s, a hideout from the police and the Bureau of Prohibition. This would have explained the floors that didn't join properly, the roof that was more like a strainer than a shield from the rain, the front steps that sagged whenever you put weight on them. It had been a rental property for college students for many, many decades; different walls had been painted and repainted, often in adventurous, nonmatching colors. The downstairs bathroom, instead of a window, had a piece of fiberglass that someone had nailed in place. It almost fit. When it snowed—which it did, off and on, for at least four months of the year—a light dusting of powder would invariably accumulate on the toilet seat.

That first night with the puppy at the cabin, Fielding realized that he would have to name his new companion. The prospect was intimidating. He considered a number of options, ranging from the traditional—Duke, Buddy, Charlie, Max—to the somewhat less traditional—Xenophon, Abercrombie, Steerforth, Waffles. Ultimately, though (after a night of perhaps somewhat less than sober-minded reflection), a single word popped into Fielding's head: *Gonker.*

It was perfect.

What did it mean? Honestly, he had no idea.

That first night, the shack in the woods held a "puppy party." Fielding's memory of the evening is hazy, but one image remains clear: a bonfire on the front lawn, and everyone dancing in a circle to "Police on My Back," by the Clash, passing Gonker back and forth, substituting the word "puppy" for "police" during the chorus.

But dogs are loyal creatures. Gonker reacted with poise to his questionable name—and surroundings. Big-pawed and big-eyed, he slept in Fielding's bed.

He was a sweet, enthusiastic dog. He had the breed's optimistic smile, the long pink tongue that readily hangs out, the occasional squint that can at times seem like a wink. The adolescent dog attended every party in the cabin; he became a mascot, a brother, an important (furry) member of the team. Golden retrievers are well known for their positive, cheerful disposition. Gonker was always standing in the doorway, it seemed, his eyebrows raised, his eyes sparkling and curious. In what is arguably his most famous speech, the nineteenth-century attorney and politician George Graham Vest described the look of Gonker, and his role in Fielding's life, perfectly: "The one absolutely unselfish friend," Vest said, "that man can have in this selfish world, the one that never deserts him, the one that never proves ungrateful or treacherous, is his dog. . . . He will kiss the hand that has no food to offer; he will lick the wounds and sores that come in encounters with the roughness of the world."

The roughness of the world. Fielding's friends, however, described it somewhat differently.

"Gonker loves keg stands!" Noel shouted one night, over the copy of *Sandinista!* that seemed to always be playing at maximum volume over the cabin's fuzzy speakers. He was pumping the tap on a silvery keg of Natural Light. "When I do them, he always barks!"

"That's because he thinks you're endangering yourself," Fielding said.

But Noel hadn't heard him; he was already upside down, nozzle between his lips, as Gonker yelped—worriedly—in the background.

One thing in particular stands out from Gonker's dissolute early years. Somewhat remarkably, Fielding and his friends taught the golden retriever to eat cookies out of their mouths. It was a sloppy business: he had prodigious salivary glands, and he'd slobber all over your face; sometimes, if you weren't careful, he'd get a piece of lip as well. Soon the cookie procedure devolved. No one was sure how or when it happened, but eventually someone discovered that Gonker would, on command, let you spit in his mouth. Then he'd swallow. Strangely, he really seemed to like it. He liked it more than the cookies.

It's unfair to speculate here about Gonker's intellectual powers. Dogs, like people, have varying preferences and idiosyncratic tastes. Perhaps he was a connoisseur of human saliva. Perhaps he could discern one person's spit from another's. Whatever the case, this became young Gonker's primary party trick—performed for either biscuits or, more commonly, pizza.

Gonker's most astonishing moment, however, might have been one Sunday morning, at three o'clock. There had been a party at the house, and the detritus was everywhere: beer bottles and dirty dishes, pizza boxes, clothes, an old car tire that someone had inexplicably brought and then left behind. Fielding had fallen asleep on the couch in the living room and, in darkness, he awoke to Gonker's frenzied barking. "Where are you?" he said, and stumbled toward the back hallway, where the noise was coming from. "What's going on?"

Fielding found Noel a few moments later—passed out, sitting propped against a wall, wearing aviator sunglasses. Gonker was barking—howling, really—just a few feet away, but Noel was insensate; he was not going to wake up. And there, maybe another five feet from both of them, in the doorway to that drafty bathroom, was a copperhead snake. In mating season, copperheads will secrete a hormone that is especially pungent—and recognizable—to dogs. This snake was coiled and alert—its triangular head totally motionless, its tail flicking back and forth. It was ready to strike.

"Noel," Fielding yelled, and grabbed his friend by the wrist. He started pulling him deeper into the darkened house. As he was being dragged, Noel awoke; he managed to half-crawl into the kitchen. And Gonker— Gonker stood there in the hallway, unmoving, close but not going any closer, barking as loud as he could at the copperhead, barking and barking and barking. "How can a people who don't mean to understand death, hope to understand love," writes John Cheever, "and who will sound the alarm?" Gonker was sounding the alarm.

13

In college, Fielding had—somewhat surprisingly—
excelled at both computer science and anthropology.
But—less surprisingly, perhaps—he struggled to find a
job immediately after his graduation. Part of the problem was actually his devotion to Gonker. "I don't want to
leave him alone at home," he told his father, in one of their
infrequent phone calls.

"I see," John said.

"He gets very lonely."

"Sure, sure."

"He needs a human presence," Fielding said.

"And a golden retriever," John said, his voice deadpan,
"does limit your job opportunities, somewhat."

In fact, no one living in that shack in the woods seemed
to find gainful employment. Soon enough, creditors were
calling.

"The power went first," Fielding recalls. "Then the
trash collection. Then the water." They started calling
their place of residence Hell House, a name that seemed
increasingly appropriate as the weeks passed. By the fall,

he and his roommates decided that it was time to take serious action.

They held a party.

Gonker featured prominently at the party, which they dubbed the "Prehistoric Keg," because of the home's lack of running water and electricity—and also because of the two kegs of beer, which Noel had labeled Neanderthal and Homo Sapiens. Gonker was dressed in a toga. Not only did he allow Fielding to wrap the bedsheet around his back and across his shoulder; he seemed to like it. He'd bark whenever anyone turned to him and said the word "caveman"—it might have been the eye contact, or perhaps a genuine understanding of comic timing. Whatever the case, the party was a success. The police didn't show up. The beer lasted through the night. In the morning, Fielding awoke on the couch in the front yard, with his head resting on Gonker's side. Though he didn't remember exactly how or when, he'd used his puppy as a pillow. Or, quite possibly, Gonker had wiggled his way into this position. Either way, Fielding patted Gonker's head, scratching behind his soft, floppy ears.

"Good boy," he whispered, and Gonker snuggled closer.

14

All good things, however, must end. At a certain point, the sheriff posted an eviction notice on their front door. A few weeks before Thanksgiving, with temperatures plummeting, Fielding called his parents.

"Mom!" he said as soon as she answered. "Great to hear your voice!"

"Who is this?" Virginia said. "I'm sorry?"

"Very funny, Mom."

Ginny and John had just sat down to dinner. John had recently retired from his position as a vice-president at Shared Medical Systems. He'd now transitioned into consulting, full-time. He had also enrolled in an M.A. program in general studies at Georgetown University—something he'd always wanted to do—for which he was reading the classics of Western thought: Locke, Hobbes, Rousseau, Jefferson. Ginny had just left her job at the Women's Center—northern Virginia's primary resource at the time for victims of sexual violence and domestic assault.

This job was—in many ways—the most important, most difficult thing she'd ever done. Founded in 1974, the Women's Center was the only place an abused woman could go for shelter in the city of McLean, and, by extension, in much of the county. But after ten years there—ten years of seeing the cycles of abuse, the relentless procession of woman after woman, in trouble and desperate and facing anguish in the home—Ginny was exhausted. She'd helped, been of assistance, aided others. She had amounted to something. Still, peace had eluded her. The dog-shaped hole in her heart remained—despite all the intervening dogs—somehow intact.

On this night, though, with this particular phone call, Virginia was enjoying herself. "I'm not hearing you clearly," she said. "Did you say you believe that I am your mother?"

"Ha-ha," Fielding said. "Joke's on me."

The post-collegiate job search moved to Washington, D.C. There were a few adjustment issues. The first happened at 4:00 a.m. the day after Fielding moved in. That morning, Virginia and John awoke to a pulsing, chugging yell—a sound not unlike a steam locomotive departing the station. It was loud. It was coming from inside the house.

"Dear God!" John said.

Virginia found her glasses and stumbled out of bed. She rushed into the hallway and toward Fielding's room and opened the door without knocking. There, on the floor, was her son.

Even after Rebecca's sudden departure, yoga had remained a part of Fielding's life. He'd been experiencing periodic stomach aches over the last few months, and yoga seemed to be a way to treat them, a kind of medicine. He'd taken to doing it as soon as he awoke, timing its practice to the conclusion of his natural sleep cycles. This often meant rising before the sun. In this case, it meant waking his parents at 4:11 a.m. with the sacred rituals of the kundalini. He'd unrolled his bright-orange neoprene mat onto the bedroom floor. Now, in his underwear, he was performing preparatory breathing exercises. Gonker stood nearby, his tail wagging happily. He liked to stretch while Fielding did the poses—occasionally joining Fielding's downward dog with his own canine interpretation.

"What," Virginia said, averting her eyes, "are you doing, Fields?"

Gonker barked.

Fielding exhaled again, a loud percussive *boom,* followed by a series of smaller, echoing gasps. "Agni Prasana," he said then, his voice unnaturally loud and echoing from his diaphragm. "Breath of Fire."

"It sounds like a death rattle," Virginia said.

"No," he said, "that was the Kabalabati."

Whatever the case, the next morning was the same. John sat up in bed this time, a look of alarm on his face. "General quarters!" he yelled. "All hands man your battle stations." The sound filled the whole upstairs, resounding through the hallways, from room to room to room.

"It's just the Agni Prasana," Ginny said, covering half

of her face with the pillow. "I don't know why you're concerned."

"We have to get him out of the house," John said.

Virginia pulled the pillow closer. "We have to get him out of the house," she said, her voice a little bit muffled by the down.

It was late 1992. The economy had just begun to inch out of recession. It was only the beginning of the prosperity of the 1990s—the first days of the tech-sector expansion. Even so, few of Fielding's friends were moving back in with their parents. He was something of an anomaly. John and Ginny were surprised as well. They'd assumed that he was on a trajectory, though precisely *what kind* of trajectory, they weren't totally sure. But they'd never expected to be sheltering their twenty-two-year-old son. Or his friendly—and somewhat dissipated—canine companion.

15

Ginny and John already had a dog, of course—a yellow Lab named Uli. After Benson, they'd hesitated to adopt again, but finally, after spending a year or two without the bichon's constant barking, they'd given in. They were a dog family; the house felt incomplete without a dog's presence.

And so: Uli. Uli was boisterous, energetic, happy—and not that bright. Often, he would wag his tail in great sweeps, launching into the air whatever happened to be on a nearby coffee table. In this way, Ginny lost priceless Meissen figurines and porcelain teacups. She lost an eighteenth-century English mantel clock. She lost a Venetian vase. She lost numerous delicate picture frames. But what could she do? It was the price of congenial—if slightly unintelligent—companionship.

Though Uli was suspicious, at first, of Gonker, his suspicion soon turned to awe, thanks primarily to the electric fence.

Ginny and John had installed the fence as a way of keeping their dogs safe: they were vigilant pet owners, always making sure that their pets didn't stray into the street. On his second night there, Virginia gave Fielding the collar for Gonker.

"No way, Mom," Fielding said. "I'm not putting that thing on him. He's wild."

"Don't be ridiculous, Fields. He's a domesticated animal."

"It's his soul, Mom," Fielding said. "His soul is wild and free."

Virginia frowned. They were standing in the kitchen, surrounded by decades of family photographs—many of which featured family pets: Benson, Thumper Dumper, Timothy, Buffy the long-haired tabby, Mr. Peepers the singing canary, even Tiny, another, short-lived family rabbit. "I just want you to do this," Virginia said. "Please do this for me."

"No way," Fielding said. "Gonker's a free spirit. He's part of the wild heart of the earth."

"Wild heart or no wild heart," Virginia said, "this is my house, Fields."

"But it's mine, too."

She paused—on the edge of something. She shook her head. "You will do this, Fielding. You must do this." But Fields had started to smile. "No," Virginia said. "Fielding, stop." Her son's spine was bending, and he was swaying back and forth. He put one foot on a chair. "Fielding Corbett Marshall, you are not to behave in that manner!"

But it was too late.

"Ooo?" he said, bending his lips into a monkey's quizzical expression. "Ooo!" he hooted. He began to sway and dance around the room, his body taking on a decidedly apelike demeanor. "Banana?" he said. "Feed ape banana? Big ape like banana."

Virginia's face was bright red. She started to say something else, but Fielding had already loped into the foyer, where he'd begun leaping over the furniture, scratching his armpits, and making loud animal noises.

Fielding called Peyton that night, from the telephone next to his old bed. Gonker lay beside him, snoring.

"I'm going crazy," he said as soon as Peyton answered. "How's college?"

"It sucks," she said. "I dressed up like a dinosaur for Halloween."

"That's cool."

"Not really," Peyton said. "There was no exposed skin. Nobody wanted to talk to me."

"I wish Mom and Dad wouldn't talk to me," Fielding said.

"And someday, Fields, your wish will come true."

"Very funny," he said. "You know what I mean."

For a moment, the lost past was alive, floating through the air, sizzling over a cross-continental phone line. Finally, Fielding sighed. "Mom wants me to collar Gonker," he said, "for the electric fence."

There was a pause on the line.

"And?" Peyton said.

"And he's not that kind of dog."

"You can't be serious."

"He won't like it. He has to be himself."

"Fields. Just put the collar on him."

"It's a major violation. It's not okay to fence his inner spirit."

"The collar doesn't go on his spirit," Peyton said.

"Okay, okay," Fielding said. "You're as bad as Mom."

And so, in the morning, Gonker was wearing a small electric transmitter around his neck. For the first few hours, it seemed to work fine. He and Uli stood out in the yard in the cold winter air, playing happily. Uli actually seemed to be showing Gonker the boundaries. They walked together to the edge of the electrified perimeter. *The bastards have us hemmed in, Commander,* Uli seemed to say. He barked. *We'll see about that,* Gonker indicated. He barked as well. Fielding checked on them a couple of times, and everything seemed to be fine.

The trouble, though, was this: the neighborhood had a fox.

Late that afternoon, the Marshalls heard frenzied barking in the yard. Virginia rushed to the dining-room window. Her hair was in rollers; she and John were attending a formal dinner party later that evening. She peered through the glass. At the end of the yard, Uli was barking as loud as he could. But he seemed to be alone. Fielding walked up behind his mother.

"Where's Gonker?" he said, peering into the yard.

And then—a flash of russet from the corner of their vision, and there Gonker was, a streaking blur of golden retriever, rushing across the lawn, heading right for the edge of the electrified perimeter. He hit it at top speed. He yelped once, his body contorting with the pain of the shock, but he didn't stop. He landed off-balance and rolled, and then he was up and on his feet again, happy, tongue hanging out of the side of his mouth. And he was off. He was chasing the fox.

Uli howled with joy. He leapt into the air, snapping at the scent of something with his jaws. He could almost taste it—the chase, the fox fur in his mouth, the instinctive pleasure of pursuit. What an incredible thing. Gonker had done it. Hooray! Hooray for Gonker! He had breached the barricade. He had fought the electric fence—and he had won.

"Oh no," Ginny said.

It took two hours to find him. At first he refused to come to them; Fielding told his parents that Gonker was always difficult to corral, even on the college quad. Eventually, though, they lured him in with a few pieces of steak. They put the steak on a plate, and, almost like magic, Gonker appeared out of the wooded land behind the house. He hadn't caught the fox, but the chase had been, quite clearly, a pleasure. Uli nuzzled him as soon as they were both back inside.

Welcome back! Uli seemed to say. Welcome back, my astonishing friend!

16

The most troubling thing about the move back to D.C., however, wasn't the struggle with parental authority, or the challenge of inhabiting, once again, a space he'd left behind. It wasn't the lack of space for Gonker to run. It wasn't the miles and miles of hot, paved, suburban roads, the glut of traffic, the hours spent battling crowds and exhaust and the difficulties—such as they were—of leaving his friends in Charlottesville. It was something quite different.

It was stomach pain—a deep cramping that started low in his abdomen and gradually spread throughout his entire gut. At first, Fielding had thought he had food poisoning, then a stomach flu. He had diarrhea; each time he stood up from the toilet, he smelled the unmistakable, coppery scent of blood.

At first, Fielding didn't reflect on the fact that he was keeping his illness a secret from his family. As it continued, though, he gradually came to realize what he was doing—and why. He knew what would happen if he told Ginny how sick he was: She'd immediately be on the phone with doctors, consulting nurses and specialists across the country. He'd become the focus of her energies, of her unquenchable needs. And, in all honesty, he just didn't know if he could handle it.

17

Each day still began, though, with the Breath of Fire, and each day, he startled his parents awake. Ginny and John took to sleeping with earplugs; after a few weeks, they installed a noise machine next to the bed.

As winter turned to spring, Fielding volunteered to help around the house. He and the dogs mowed the lawn together, with Gonker and Uli running beside the mower, barking and wagging their tails. Halfway through, however, Ginny came rushing out of the front door.

"Fields—what are you doing?" she cried. "Stop!"

"What do you mean?"

"Are you mowing letters into the lawn?"

He looked at what he'd done. A large "G" for "Gonker," followed by a "U" for "Uli," and an "F" for "Fielding." G U F.

"Sure," he said, frowning. "But it'll all flatten out."

"The grain of the mower!" Ginny said. "It'll be visible for weeks!"

He also had dubious bathing and sartorial habits. His tie-dyed tank top was his uniform, and he would revel in the scent of his own sweat, which—his yogi had convinced him—was the holy odor of the holy body. He would add some patchouli to the mix, just to balance everything out. He surrounded himself with a cloud of *Fielding*. And though he hadn't taken a vow of celibacy, between his attention to the job search, his daily practice of yoga, and his woodsy odor, the point was mostly moot.

One evening, the Marshalls had two of their friends from the neighborhood, the Millers, over for dinner. Fielding appeared halfway through the meal, having just gone for a jog. He was wearing the tank top and reeked of perspiration. "Sugar Magnolia" echoed at high volume from his headphones. He nodded to the dinner guests and— humming along—took his father's water glass and drank the icy liquid down.

"Ah," he said, misjudging how loud his voice should have been. "That hits the spot."

Mr. Miller put his hand on his water glass.

"I think you're safe," John said. "Although you can never tell."

Ginny turned toward Mrs. Miller's side of the table. "He's always been a free spirit," she said, *sotto voce*.

However, even as Virginia's exasperation with her son increased, she grew closer to her son's dog. She loved the way Gonker would sit at the picture window in the kitchen, watching the bluebirds in the backyard. He'd track them as they darted between the nesting box and the suet feeder. Once, Fielding caught him sitting there, his paws crossed, his head held high, his white ascot fluffed and regal—and a single, long rope of drool hanging from one side of his mouth.

"He's imagining a bluebird sandwich," Fielding said.

"Nonsense," Virginia said. "The bluebirds are a thing of beauty and Gonker knows it."

"A beautiful sandwich," Fielding said. "He knows they'd be delicious."

To Virginia, however, this was impossible. To her, he was simply enjoying the manifold wonder of the natural world. He was appreciative, not hungry. She even began putting videos of birds on the television in the kitchen—something for him to watch while she cleaned the kitchen, or read on the sun porch. He seemed to like anything colorful—a cardinal, a blue jay, a goldfinch. This agreed with Ginny's sensibilities: she'd always loved ornamentation and brightly plumed birds, and she took great joy in the beauty of nature. It was a reminder of how nature could stand apart from people's brutality and thoughtlessness.

She would cook for Gonker, too. She delighted in this role, providing him with a range of meaty meals—mostly based on ground beef. And, more than any other single activity, Gonker loved to eat. Almost anything could be a welcome snack. He was an indiscriminate eater—not a gourmet, but a gourmand. A big dog, he could eat an entire pie in a few bites, which he did whenever someone made the mistake of leaving one unattended. Almost nothing was safe; once, Virginia awoke to a noise down-stairs in the kitchen; when she investigated, she discovered three cans of tuna fish, all of them punctured by small canine teeth, sucked dry of their fish juice. Gonker was standing nearby. When he saw Virginia start to clean up the mess, he just put his head down and, averting his eyes, slunk slowly away, his tail between his legs in his shame.

Gonker filled the house with his energy. He would greet Virginia, John, and Fielding at the door—every single time they came home—with joyous enthusiasm, smil-ing his crooked smile, spinning in circles on the hardwood floor of the entryway. He'd wait at the base of the stairs, wait for Virginia to put on his plaid sweater vest. Once it was on—only then did he seem truly happy.

His favorite activity—once he'd been "vested"—was the chasing of sticks. He kept a collection of them beside the front door, and before he went outside for a walk, he would begin the process of selecting just the right one. It was a process that could take several minutes. Once the appropriate stick was secure, he would leap forward, straining at the leash, leading you forward.

If you agreed to play fetch with him, it could be an hour-long commitment. He'd persist long after the game had ended, pushing his nose against you, leaning on you, reminding you that you'd somehow—through some almost unimaginable oversight—left a game of fetch, in progress.

"Fetch?" he seemed to say, nudging you again and again. "Fetch? Fetch? Fetch?"

Then he'd bark, and sprint off a little ways, and pantomime the retrieval of an imaginary stick. He'd return it and stand there, tongue hanging out of the side of his mouth, waiting for you to understand. If you failed to join him in the game, he'd try the whole procedure again. He was indefatigable.

Ginny began to think of Gonker as a kind of spy; prone to covert activity, he seemed always to be planning something. But—he would never be caught. One night, he went downstairs with the family willingly, or what appeared to be willingly, after dinner. The Marshalls were watching a movie. It was an engrossing action film, one that began with a chase scene. After thirty minutes or so, Ginny pulled her attention away from the screen and said, "Where's Gonker?"

The most impressive thing wasn't that he'd opened the lid to the trash can, or that he'd removed the bag of trash and taken the trash apart carefully, sorting it into categories: edible in one area, paper in another, metal in a third. It was a meticulous job, really, and he'd done it quite well. But most impressive was that, after devouring everything he could, he'd carefully closed the door to the trash, and arranged himself on his dog bed in the kitchen. He looked angelic, innocent. "Did you see the guy who made this mess?" he seemed to be saying. "About this tall, this wide. Yellow coat. Real sneaky-looking. I'll let you know if he comes by again."

———

Like Oji, Gonker seemed to sense when his owner most needed his compassion. When Fielding was napping—feeling ill during the middle of the day—Gonker would rally Uli to the cause. They'd both bolt into Fielding's bedroom, jump on the bed at once, and bark at him, as loud as they could. Two dogs barking at you in a bed—it will change your outlook on the day in a hurry.

Sometimes Gonker would find Fielding—at his moments of deepest suffering—in the bathroom, bent over in pain, clutching his stomach, his insides rebelling, filling with a kind of fire. This called for Uli as well, but a silent Uli. And so the two dogs would edge up to Fielding in this circumstance, and they would start to sniff and lick him—his ankle, his knee, his shoulder, and, eventually, his face. Two dogs licking your face quietly will have much the same effect as two dogs barking at you in a bed.

One Saturday during that first year together, Virginia was baking a loaf of bread from scratch. After she proofed the dough, she left it sitting in an earthenware bowl on the kitchen counter, slowly rising.

At some point after dinner, Uli began behaving strangely.

"Why's he barking so much?" Virginia said.

The Marshalls went into the foyer, where Uli was waiting. He ran circles around them—acting like a dog possessed.

"What's going on, Uli?" John said.

He was—they would soon discover—a decoy. They heard a loud crash in the kitchen; by the time everyone made it in there to see what had happened, Ginny's bowl was in pieces on the tile floor, and the dough had disappeared. Gonker was licking his lips, a satisfied expression on his face. Uli barked with pride at their accomplishment.

And yet.

A dog's stomach—it turns out—is an ideal environment for yeast to multiply. As yeast multiplies, it needs energy. In this case, the yeast ate all of the sugars in the still-raw bread dough. And then the yeast produced two notable by-products: carbon dioxide and alcohol. Gonker's stomach had become a brewery.

Soon he was belching and farting uncontrollably and stumbling around the house, as his body absorbed the booze that the yeast was producing.

"Call the vet," Ginny said. "Call Great Falls Animal Hospital."

Uli, unaware that anything was amiss, stood nearby, panting and wagging his tail.

"He's fine," Fielding said. "He's had much more to drink—believe me."

"He could die, Fields."

"He's not going to die."

Fielding walked over to Gonker and sat down on the floor. He put his hands under Gonker's meaty shoulders and lifted the dog onto his lap. He felt Gonker settle into him. He felt him shift uncomfortably, for a moment, and then—fall asleep.

"See," Fielding said, looking up at his mother. "He's sleeping like a baby."

"A drunken baby," John said.

"It's a family tradition," Ginny said, sardonically. And then: "I'm going to call the vet myself."

"Please don't, Mom," Fielding said.

"I'm just concerned about his welfare."

"Not to mention his moral fiber," John said.

Virginia dialed the animal hospital from the phone in the kitchen and put her son on the line. Dogs, of course, *can* die from eating raw bread dough. Fielding was astonished when the veterinarian told him this. Virginia could see the color drain from her son's face as he had a long, serious conversation with the vet. She walked over and put her hand on Fielding's head, brushing the hair away from his face, out of his eyes. Fielding hung up. He glanced at his parents.

"We're supposed to watch him closely," he said, "to see if he vomits."

"Not too closely, I hope," John said.

But Gonker was fine, although next morning, Fielding noticed, he didn't seem as enthusiastic as usual for his daily walk. Fielding himself was feeling a little nauseous that morning. "You and me both," Fielding whispered to his dog. "What a pair we are."

Ginny went into Fielding's room that night to check on

Gonker. He wagged his tail when he saw her but didn't lift up his head. She sat down next to him. "Old friend," she said, softening her voice, "you feel poorly today?" She petted his body carefully, making sure that her touch was gentle. "A bit hungover, maybe?" He wagged his tail some more. "One second," she said. "I'll be right back."

She went downstairs and took a Ziploc bag of chicken soup from the freezer, defrosted it in the microwave, and carried it upstairs. Gonker was on his feet as soon as he smelled it. He began lapping it up even before she put the dish on the floor—taking in the electrolytes and hydration his body so badly needed. His tongue licked the bottom of the bowl, the sides of the bowl, the carpet all around the bowl. He looked at her with gratitude. "Another round?" Ginny asked; Gonker narrowed his eyes and, rolling down onto his back, sighed and seemed to nod.

18

When do you treat a symptom? When do you go to the doctor? When do you let someone else know what you're going through, especially if the symptom is humiliating? When do you break through the walls you've built between yourself and those closest to you—if that break could help save your life? All Fielding knew was that he was ill and his body seemed to be constantly in revolt. He went to the library reference section and got a medical dictionary; the list of illnesses that his pain could indicate was long, and fearsome.

Some nights, he felt light-headed from the loss of blood. Even more difficult to manage was the pain. He started avoiding regular mealtimes, began denying himself food. The only thing that felt normal was this: an empty stomach, empty of everything except water. Water felt sustaining; it felt vital and alive. So he would take his portion of food up to his room at night and feed it to Gonker, scratching Gonker's ears while he fed him dinner off of the family's good dinner plates. "That's it, fella," he'd say, "eat up." *God knows I can't.* He took great solace in Gonker's appetite, as if he was able to eat vicariously, through his dog.

Fielding began to lose weight. He'd plan to visit a specialist, or to tell his parents what he was going through, to give in to the onslaught of parental care. But then, right when he'd made up his mind to do either of these things, the symptoms would briefly abate. He'd begin to doubt them, somehow. And he remained stubbornly resistant. He wanted to keep his personal life—his adult personal life—to himself.

If you compared the relationship between Virginia and her mother with the relationship that Virginia had built with her son, there's no question which was stronger. Yet it is difficult sometimes to trust the people who are closest to you, to trust them in ways beyond the ways you've grown accustomed to trusting them. For his part, Fielding felt harassed by his parents, who so badly wanted him to find employment. This became, in fact, the center of their relationship: an ongoing monologue about career prospects. It made him unlikely to extend the relationship further, to bridge it into another part of his life.

"Why don't you call our friend Paul Perrot?" Virginia would suggest. "He has a cousin who programs computers; he works for General Electric, and I'm sure he could find you something there." Or: "You should be going on informational interviews, Fielding, don't you think?" Or: "It might be the way you dress, Fielding. Can your father and I buy you a suit?" Or: "From those to whom much is given, Fields, much is expected." Or: "As a Myers-Briggs

ESFP, you'll have to work harder on self-discipline. Let's make some charts and lists to help you with your planning process."

He had a number of short-lived tech jobs through a temp agency. But he approached these contract positions halfheartedly. Besides the illness, they all separated him from Gonker, which made them, for one reason or another, inadequate. He'd taken to talking with the dog—though he didn't know it—much as his own mother had talked with Oji.

"What do you think, Gonker?" Fielding would say. "Should we apply to grad school in anthropology?"

Or: "What do I really want to do this weekend?"

Or: "Do I want to try and get that job at RadioShack?"

Though this began as a sort of joke, it actually became a way for Fielding to sort through his more complicated problems. Phrasing a question aloud made it necessary to articulate it in words—and this articulation was surprisingly difficult sometimes. Gonker, of course, didn't provide any answers. He'd just narrow his eyes, pant, and look at Fielding with pleasant optimism. He'd smile. Yet this was useful. The smile, especially, was reassuring.

At one of the temporary tech jobs, Fielding set up a primitive Webcam—perhaps the first in northern Virginia. Fielding could use his connection—dial-up on both sides—to download a feed of Gonker, its images taken in three-second intervals, and to send Gonker, in turn, a feed of himself, also taken in three-second intervals. Gonker reacted with mild curiosity to the images of Fielding. His side of it, though, was funny to watch. Gonker would stagger across the screen whenever he moved, a caricature of a stop-animation dog.

When Fielding was most ill during these months—as the illness cycled in and out, becoming a crisis and then abating somewhat—he noticed something unusual. Gonker's dish, which he kept on the floor in the kitchen, was almost always empty by nighttime. But when Fielding wasn't able to stomach food, Gonker could somehow tell, and he, too, began to refuse food. He'd leave his meal untouched.

"Come on, boy," Fielding would say, sitting in his chair. "Dinnertime."

But nothing could entice the golden retriever to consume his kibble. He'd only stand there and look at the food impassively, look over at Fielding, and wait.

Finally, one day in March 1995, Fielding came home with news.

"I got a full-time job," he told his parents, "at a start-up downtown."

"Hallelujah!" Ginny said.

"Tranquillity Base here!" John exclaimed. "The Eagle has landed!"

In a phone call that night with Peyton, Fielding expressed his chief worry about the future: "They won't let me take him to work except on Fridays."

"The dog will survive, Fields."

"But what if he's lonely?"

"Do you want to live with Mom and Dad forever?" Peyton said. "'As a Myers-Briggs ESFP,'" she added, mimicking their mother's voice, "'perhaps you'll find comfort in some extroverted, improvised behavior.'"

"Got it," Fielding said.

"Maybe you could send the dog to work," Peyton said, "on your behalf? He might be more effective."

"Thanks a lot."

"He'd certainly smell better, that's for sure."

"I love you, too, sis," Fielding said.

19

The Marshall household became quieter without a son and a son's dog. Uli, for his part, seemed sad to see his companion go. They'd managed to chase away three mailmen, one UPS delivery driver, and one teenager who was selling raffle tickets for his band. Fortunately, no one had complained—or called the proper authorities.

There was a larger problem, however. The lingering effect of the bread incident was that Virginia Marshall had begun to worry about Gonker's health. She felt that he needed better care. Fielding just didn't seem mature enough to really care for his dog. If Gonker could break through an electric fence and eat a bowl of bread dough in the relative safety of Virginia's clean and orderly home, well, there was just no telling what might happen wherever Fielding might move next. Every aspect of Gonker's care became part of the ongoing narrative of Fielding's relationship with his mother. When Fielding found an apartment in West Falls Church—just behind a Food Lion and a Dunkin' Donuts—Virginia pushed for assurances that Gonker would still make it regularly to the vet.

"Of course he will, Mom."

"And you'll get his teeth cleaned?"

"Of course I will."

"And you'll get him groomed? He loves to be clean and well combed."

"Mom."

"Will you do it?"

"Yes, Mom."

"He's such a sweet little guy."

"He weighs sixty-five pounds," Fielding said. "Now—with the doughnuts—even more."

Gonker loved doughnuts. He would eat them in a particular way—a way that astonished Fielding the first time he did it. He'd push the doughnut along the ground until he was able to get the tip of his nose inside of it. He'd flick his head upward, throwing the doughnut into the air, then look up and catch it in his mouth as it fell. *Delicious.*

He seemed to learn the names of the flavors, as well. He liked Cinnamon Sugar above all the others. And when Fielding said to him, in a certain tone of voice, "Cinnamon Sugar?" he would bark enthusiastically.

Dunkin' Donuts was, however, the highlight of living in West Falls Church. This was a different kind of suburb, but a suburb nonetheless. Three stops from the end of the D.C. Metro Orange Line, it was a vast paved world of parking lots and strip malls and chain restaurants. Late-twentieth-century American mall culture was perhaps most clearly articulated in West Falls Church, circa 1995. Every commodity was a reproduction of some other commodity, somewhere else. You could be *there*—at Applebee's or Chili's or Ross Dress for Less—or you could be in suburban Omaha. Or suburban San Diego. Or suburban Fort Lauderdale. The visual landscape would be the same. Even the odors were sprayed through the air by the gallon. Though Gonker refrained from judgment, Fielding found himself yearning for the Charlottesville past, for the Hell House and its acres of empty woods. For its keg stands. For the fact that, almost certainly, no one would *try* to replicate that cabin, anywhere else in the world. And so, one Friday night, he called Noel.

Noel had never left Charlottesville; he was playing bass in a bluegrass-jazz fusion band, taking odd jobs. "Hey, dude," Noel said when he answered. "What's up? I'm just eating a pizza."

"Not much," Fielding said. "How's life treating you?"

"Amazing, bro," Noel said. "Incredible. I just, like, played softball all week."

"You mean this weekend?" Fielding said.

"No, man. All week. Like, we started this game on Monday, and, like, we just were playing, you know, and we got to the end of the day, but nobody could remember what inning it was, right? And so we just started again the next day." He paused. "We did that a few times."

Fielding sighed. He was sitting in the chair on his apartment's tiny balcony, a balcony that overlooked the neon-lit parking lot and the flickering yellow sign for NAPA Auto Parts. He'd spent the day in a cubicle, writing lines of code in JavaScript—a programming language that he'd managed to teach himself. Now, feeling vaguely nauseous, he was sitting next to Gonker and idly patting the dog's head.

"How high were you?" Fielding asked.

"Oh, man," Noel said. "Wow."

Fielding shook his head. "Good to know," he said, "that nothing's really changed."

20

Months passed. On July 4, 1995, Fielding returned home for a visit. Ginny spent the week preparing for her son's arrival: she made his bed, bought a box of dog treats at the store, began making an elaborate meal for the family.

Fielding drove up on the morning of the holiday, feeling weak and hollowed out. When he opened the door, Gonker climbed out of the car. Usually, Gonker was all energy and enthusiasm—barely controllable. But this was a changed dog. When Gonker saw Uli, he didn't bound toward him. He merely panted a little, and seemed to smile in greeting. The two dogs actually walked out into the yard and sat on the grass. Gonker lay down and rested his head on his paws.

Concerned, Ginny brought two bowls of kibble outside. Uli devoured his, but Gonker left his untouched. Uli walked over to him, nudged his friend with his nose. Gonker didn't move. Uli walked back to the dish and stood over it, nervously. He glanced back at Gonker and then settled down beside his companion's dinner, guarding it for him.

"Something's wrong, Fields," Virginia said, standing in the doorway, looking toward the garden.

"He's just hot."

"He hasn't touched his food."

Fielding frowned. "He's fine."

But Ginny was concerned. She had grown to love Gonker—had missed him, in fact—and seeing him appear uncomfortable caused her chest to tighten. It was visceral, a hand that gripped her and squeezed.

Fielding felt unsteady on his feet. That day, he'd only eaten an apple and a carrot. He was experimenting with a raw diet, to see if this would give him some relief. He knelt down next to his companion. He ruffled his golden fur.

"We're just a little under the weather," he said to him. "Right?"

Virginia shook her head. "Not this," she said. "This is more."

John came up and stood behind the two of them. "That," he said, "is one sick animal."

It's a tribute to the dog's big heart that he seemed okay to his owner. Gonker was ill—but Fielding couldn't see it. Whenever Fielding approached him, Gonker would get up, wag his tail, and try to act happy and normal—to seem like his old self. He'd summon whatever energy reserves he possessed and make a gigantic effort to act like a typical dog. Now he rolled over and seemed to smile at Fielding. He nuzzled his owner's palm, just for a moment. But then, after only a second, his eyes closed, and he seemed to lapse into unconsciousness. Fielding glanced over at his mother, indicating that he was now getting nervous—that maybe something unusual *was* wrong with his companion. And as it turned out, Gonker was in fact quite sick.

21

In 1855, Dr. Thomas Addison first described Addison's disease, a disorder of the adrenal glands that, if untreated, is fatal. It is a condition that afflicts both humans and animals.

Those suffering from Addison's disease are never far from crisis; they could, at any moment, experience its debilitating effects. With Addison's, the body fails to produce enough glucocorticoids. And without glucocorticoids, you enter a state that's known as adrenal insufficiency. You have debilitating pain, your blood pressure plummets, you struggle to stay conscious, and then—if you don't get medication—you lapse into a coma and die. It can be quite fast, and quite grisly, but with modern synthetic medicines it can be readily controlled.

John F. Kennedy was an Addisonian. His personal physician was summoned to the White House a number of times to monitor his episodes. Kennedy took medication to conceal his symptoms, but they persisted nonetheless, causing him great pain. At some of the key moments of his presidency, he was having up to six injections of medication a day—many of which were the steroids he needed to stay alive. And Kennedy was not the only well-known Addisonian. Modern researchers have speculated that it was this condition, undiagnosed, that killed Jane Austen, robbing her first of her eyesight, then her ability to walk, and, finally, her life.

On the night of that Fourth of July, Gonker hid under the bed. He couldn't be lured out; he wanted only to lie in darkness. The next day, Virginia finally persuaded Fielding to take Gonker in. She and John accompanied their son to the clinic. The Marshalls drove somberly to Great Falls Animal Hospital, with Gonker sprawled across Fielding's lap in the back seat.

As soon as Dr. Henshaw saw Gonker's symptoms, he ordered a blood test. The results came back within an hour.

"Addison's disease?" Fielding said. "I've never heard of it."

Dr. Henshaw hurried to reassure them that it was serious but that, with managed care, it probably wouldn't be fatal. Gonker shuddered. He moved around on the floor of the examination room as if he couldn't get comfortable.

"Can you do anything for the pain?" Fielding asked. "For right now?"

"We just need to see how he reacts to the medicine," Dr. Henshaw explained. "But first you have to make a decision." He paused, then explained that there were two options available to Fielding but he had to choose quickly. He could treat Gonker with pills or with an injection. Fielding would have to give him one pill every day, but this would still be far less costly than the injection, administered every four weeks in the vet's office, under the careful supervision of a clinician.

"What would you do," Fielding asked, "if Gonker was your dog?"

The vet squinted at him, narrowing his eyes and creasing his forehead. His look was calculated and careful. "Me?" he said. "I don't know. That has to be your decision. But whatever you choose—it will demand vigilance." He paused. "Attentiveness."

Fielding looked down at Gonker, who was now whimpering and shaking. Within the past twenty minutes, he'd started licking the sides of his own muzzle, again and again. Fielding knew that in dogs this was often a sign of fear. Was he afraid, Fielding wondered, of the way his own body was feeling?

"Give him the injection," he said. "Let's start right now."

Dr. Henshaw nodded. He left the room momentarily and then returned with a long syringe filled with yellow fluid. "The next twenty-four hours," he said, "will tell us everything we need to know."

"So he might be too far gone?" Virginia asked.

"I don't think so," Dr. Henshaw said. "Not yet. But you should probably say goodbye now," he said, "just in case." Then he turned and gave Gonker the shot. The dog didn't even seem to notice. Afterward, the vet stopped to stroke Gonker's ears. "Too many episodes," he concluded, "could have a cumulative effect. He might get too weak to recover."

He'd been speaking to Virginia here, and so she cleared her throat.

"Gonker," she said, "belongs to my son."

Dr. Henshaw looked over to Fielding, addressing him alone. "When he's well again, don't think he's cured. People often make this mistake." He waited for his words to sink in, for Fielding to nod and signal that he'd understood. "There is no cure," he added. "He'll need monthly injections and your watchful care for the rest of his life."

22

After Gonker's first injection of synthetic hormones, however, he slowly began to improve. For several weeks, Fielding had to feed him by hand, cooking all of Gonker's meals himself, giving the golden retriever nothing but fresh organic food.

"Here you go, buddy," he'd say. "Organic, grass-fed, and free-range."

Gonker, it should be noted, seemed to appreciate the effort. As the hormones accumulated in his blood, he gradually regained his energy. He started to look at the birds, once again, with hunger. His long-term prognosis, the vet indicated on his first return visit, was decent. As long as he received his regular injections of synthetic cortisol, prednisone, and fludrocortisone acetate, his health would probably deteriorate no further.

Once, when Fielding and Gonker were visiting, Ginny wrapped a box and gave it to Gonker; inside, ingeniously, was a single-serving pie—a gift any dog would love. Fielding watched Gonker rip the package open with his teeth and claws. The pie was apple—his favorite. Gonker chewed on it contentedly, lying in front of the family hearth, where a succession of Marshall pets had slept over the years. Ginny, at some point, came in to sit next to her son. They watched Gonker sleep. They didn't say anything at all.

23

When a dog depends on you, you depend on it—the exchange is never one-sided. There is something fundamental about caring for an animal; it opens you to stewardship, to quietude, to grace. It is a long, slow relationship, built on a thousand daily actions. Wake up, prepare the food, go on the walk, return home, prepare the food, go on the walk.

In his small, magical book, *Creaturely and Other Essays,* Devin Johnston stitches together a series of essays about animals—animals that live in, or on the margins of, our human world. City dwellers, all of them: dogs, starlings, crows, squirrels, mice. He walks his border collie, Chester, through the neighborhoods of St. Louis; this walking gives him access to the city at all hours of the day and night; this access, in turn, gives him the structure for a book. The essays themselves loop around numerous themes, but the presence of animals in our lives—often unseen, unconsidered, unnoticed—is something he returns to, again and again. Out in Tower Grove Park in central St. Louis, Johnston is watching an owl: "I shift ten paces to the right and raise my binoculars: the owl's unblinking eyes remain fixed on me, chrome yellow around the pupils. I am more watched than watcher."

I am more watched than watcher. How crucial to our well-being are the dogs who live in our midst? Go outside, look around any dog park, and you'll see it—humans congregated together, seemingly worry-free, taking photographs of themselves and their dogs, compiling albums and albums of carefree images that provide a respite from the pressures of adulthood—an invitation to explore, to imagine. Modern life can feel technologically overwhelming, always. Where is the time to rest? Dogs offer it to us—if we'll take it—each and every day.

The Internet is flooded with videos of moments when we set aside our consciousness in order simply to *be* with animals: Videos of dogs greeting soldiers returning from war. Or videos of animals being rescued from abuse. Or of people saving animals—a Russian man, for example, who breaks through an icy pond with his fists in order to save a black Lab. These are moments of simple action, easy presence. To use a term borrowed from yoga, *vinyasa.* Present, continuous action linked to breath. Or, as Elizabeth Gilbert writes in *Eat, Pray, Love,* "A place of eternal presence from which you may regard yourself and your surroundings with poise."

On that first night back safely at their apartment, Gonker sat at the foot of Fielding's bed, in his customary spot, curled up in his dog basket. And yet Fielding still felt a puzzling sense of loss. He fell asleep only after a long struggle. His dreams were fitful. In them, he wandered through an empty landscape, looking for something he'd misplaced but couldn't quite visualize or even name. And—as often still happened in his dreams—there was Rebecca. She appeared out of the emptiness and was walking beside him.

"You lost me," she told him. "You couldn't make me stay."

He sat up, startled, wide-eyed, and saw the morning sunlight coming through the window. On the mattress next to him was Gonker, who'd joined him in the night. And while he was having nightmares, Fielding had clutched handfuls of the dog's fur. Gonker's golden hair was still threaded through his fingers. But the dog was comfortably asleep.

PART 4

The Flea and the Lion

RAMBURES

> That island of England breeds very valiant creatures;
> their mastiffs are of unmatchable courage.

DUKE OF ORLEANS

> Foolish curs, that run winking into the mouth of a
> Russian bear and have their heads crushed like rotten
> apples! You may as well say, that's a valiant flea that dare
> eat his breakfast on the lip of a lion.

CONSTABLE

> Just, just; and the men do sympathize with the mastiffs in
> robustious and rough coming on, leaving their wits with
> their wives: and then give them great meals of beef and
> iron and steel, they will eat like wolves and fight like devils.
>
> —SHAKESPEARE, *Henry V*, Act III, Scene VII

24

On October 10, 1998, if you'd been in a plane looking down over the Appalachian Trail, perhaps you would have seen a little speck of yellow making its furious way among the trees. Perhaps, too, you would have seen Fielding standing up from the mud and finding Noel. The two of them searching and yelling for Gonker, as darkness began to settle in around them.

Fielding fell again, this time slipping on the moss-covered boards of a bridge, tumbling over its side and into a streambed. He'd cut his shins badly—both of them—and so the blood had run until it scabbed, the wounds clotting with mud and grass. They'd searched into the night—wandering, pacing back and forth, calling Gonker's name—the only two figures in an empty autumn landscape.

After ten o'clock—at the Denny's in Salem, Virginia—they sat and discussed what had happened. Fielding was too sick to eat anything, but he'd ordered a coffee—more to have something to hold on to, something to look at so he wouldn't cry.

"You did all you could, dude," Noel said. "We weren't going to find him in the dark."

This was likely true. But somehow Fielding felt that he should have worked harder—that he should have done more. He said nothing. He just sat there in silence, holding the coffee cup and staring down at the steaming black liquid. He let the condensation collect on his skin; he could feel the heat of it begin to burn him—but he didn't move.

In McLean, John and Ginny had cooked a light dinner and put a CD on: Mozart's *Magic Flute,* one of Virginia's favorites.

The sound of the choir filled the house with its disembodied, floating hosanna. Virginia had a glass of iced tea, and they sat down to read on the spacious sun porch, with its view of the forestland behind the house. The Marshall residence is full of mechanical clocks, many of them antiques from all over the world, and they are timed to go off in sequence, their chimes staggered so that, over a ten-minute period surrounding the top of each hour, the sound of bells cascades throughout the ground floor of the home.

John and Ginny's conversation ranged widely, moving, as it usually did, from work to friends to family. Ginny got up and returned to the kitchen, where she refilled her glass. The phone rang. She paused there, near the dining-room table, iced tea in one hand. She looked at the ringing phone, hesitating, deliberating. Finally, just before the machine answered, she reached her hand out.

That moment would forever linger in Ginny's memory; she would always be able to summon the feeling of the receiver against her palm, the scent of the kitchen after dinner, the faint sounds of "Alles fühlt der liebe Freuden" in the background. "Marshall residence," she said, wondering who would be calling at nearly 11:00 p.m.

It was Fielding. *Oh no,* Ginny thought as soon as she heard his voice.

A trace of fear shot through her body, visceral and cold.

25

Standing there in her kitchen, talking to Fielding, Ginny kept repeating the word "lost," again and again, asking him to describe the day in detail, to relive every step. Without her willing it, fifty years were collapsing, falling completely away. Suddenly Virginia was a girl again— weeping in the driveway of her home, looking for Oji, calling and calling him, over and over and over, without response, with only silence.

She kept asking Fielding to retell his morning because she wanted to be able to put herself there, to locate herself at the scene of the disappearance. If she could only do this, then she could get some kind of clearer sense of what had happened. She'd be able to see it. And then maybe, just maybe, she could begin to understand. But there was nothing—no realization, no understanding, no explanation—only loss. As she listened, something built inside of her, some kind of deep and unruly emotion, something from a distant, buried past.

"I knew this would happen," she said. "I just knew

it." She ran her hands through her hair, massaging her forehead with her fingertips. She didn't know where this anger—this rage—was coming from. "I just don't understand it, Fielding. What—what is wrong with you?"

But as soon as she said these words, she regretted them deeply. He'd just been himself, and nothing else. He was her son. Her duty was to protect him, to support him, to love him—not to tear him down. And so Virginia apologized, again and again, saying that it was just bad luck, that it was uncontrollable—that it was no one's fault. But at some fundamental level, she believed otherwise. She felt a deep and abiding shame—something that had harnessed her since her childhood. Every failure in her life, she believed, was her own. She was—somehow—the one to hold responsible. She should have been more vigilant. She should have been in control. She should have seen something like this coming.

When Fielding came over the next night, the Marshalls sat in the living room and drank coffee. When a loss hits a family, it doesn't make sense. The absence of a loved one—whoever it is—just sits there, hangs in the air when everyone is together, looming over and around everyone, making them all aware of it, even if they're not thinking about it directly.

"I can do it," Fielding finally said. He'd washed his face but he hadn't changed his mud-stained clothes.

The knee of his jeans had torn when he'd fallen down the embankment of the ravine. He was wide-eyed. He'd barely slept—and he'd gone back out in the morning, too. "Work doesn't matter. I'll drive up there tonight. My boss can fire me if he wants to."

"No!" Virginia and John chorused, much too vehemently. They exchanged a quick glance.

"What we mean is," John continued, "that you need to get your rest."

But Fielding shook his head.

"I left my shirt for him to find," he said. "I have to go back. I have to show him I'm coming back."

Uli walked over to Fielding and stood in front of him, panting slightly, looking up at his face. Uli wondered what was going on. Where was Gonker? Why was Fielding here? Had he brought doughnuts?

"Fielding," Virginia said, "you're overexcited." She recognized the shadow of breakdown in her son's demeanor. His eyes were bloodshot and red; his breathing was rushed and ragged. He couldn't seem to calm down. "Let me get you a glass of water," she added. "Do you want ice?"

Parents love their children in a multitude of ways. Parents can be distant, or they can be affectionate and close. They can be kind; they can, of course, be brutal. There is no such thing, really, as the story of a child; there is only the story of a parent and a child, and the ways the parent built, or destroyed, or relinquished the bond with the child.

In trauma-survival groups, it is common for survivors to fill out a checklist to see how grave parental wounding is:

- I was not cherished and celebrated by my parents simply by virtue of my existence. I thought I had to be different or perform to be accepted.
- I did not have the experience of being a "delight" to my parents and those around me.
- I did not hear affirmation—words of acceptance and validation.
- I did not hear my mom or dad say, "I love you."
- I did not have a parent that took time to understand me or encourage me to share who I was: what I felt, what I needed and what I wanted.

These are the first five questions of the Mother/Father Wound assessment, a common diagnostic instrument. They were something that Virginia Marshall carried with her, in her subconscious, at all times. They were the questions she sought to escape; they pointed to the devastation that she wanted, so deeply, not to inflict. She was haunted, not just by the neglect she'd suffered, but by the fear that she might do the same thing to her own children. She was afraid that, despite her best and focused efforts, she would repeat her own wounding.

Ginny came back in from the kitchen, a large, beaded water glass in her hand. She handed it wordlessly to her son. After a few moments, Fielding said: "Didn't you lose a dog, Dad?"

"Everybody loses a dog," John said.

"Did you find him?"

"Not exactly," John said, making significant eye contact with Virginia. "But that's not the important thing to remember. The important thing to remember is not to get discouraged."

"Gonker's lost in the Appalachian Mountains, Dad."

"Anything is within your power, Fielding."

"It's a million square miles."

"The human intellect is boundless in its capacity for innovation—" John began, but Fielding cut him off.

"I know, Dad, I know."

"Fielding," Virginia said suddenly, "when was the last time Gonker had his shot?"

The shot. Fielding thought, and flashed back to that decision he'd made—seemingly inconsequential at the time—to choose the shot instead of the pills. If he'd chosen the pills, he now realized, Gonker would have at most a few more days left.

Before he could answer her, though, Ginny walked to the kitchen. She pulled the family calendar off the wall. Yes—there it was. She'd marked the date of Gonker's last injection on it: ten days ago.

"He has about twenty days left," Ginny said, turning back toward her family. She sat down at the table, staring at the precise and orderly grid of the month. Gonker would next need his medicine on November 1.

"That's not even three weeks," Fielding said.

But Virginia was silent. When Gonker had first gotten sick, she'd asked Great Falls Animal Hospital what might exacerbate his condition. The veterinarian's words came back to her now, a vivid memory: "Certainly stress can do it," he'd said. Stress could shorten the interval. If the dog was threatened in any way, he would need his medicine sooner.

26

This is a dog.

Small and sweet, this avatar—an image of something that so many of us love, beyond reason, beyond comprehension.

A yellow dog.

If he is wet, he reeks like week-old flower water.

If he is frightened, he can bite.

If he is hungry, he eats almost anything—living or dead.

If he is curious about something, he puts his nose in it.

If he is tired, he sleeps where he is tired.

If he is happy?

He is always happy. Or almost always.

If he is lost?

He needs—above all else—human kindness.

27

It's tough to conceive of the world that existed fifteen years ago, when the Web was new—when there were no iPhones, no GPS in your pocket, no Facebook, no Twitter, no affinity-based message boards, no lost-dog apps for Android *or* Apple. When Virginia Marshall had a serious problem in 1998, a crisis within the family, she didn't look anything up online. She didn't go to Craigslist. In fact, she turned to that millennia-old technology: the map.

She still has it, to this day—the big foldable map of the state of Virginia. Two days after Gonker disappeared, Ginny found a big Rand McNally map of the state—folded and stuffed in the back of a drawer under the microwave. She took it out and spread it across the kitchen table. A map of the state that bore her name, with its arterial tangle of interstates and small highways, its clear demarcations of counties and towns and the natural, external world.

The area of the Blue Ridge Parkway where Gonker had been lost was almost two hundred miles outside of D.C. Ginny closed her eyes and tried to picture it. She remembered it as intimidating, a smear of green mountains—hot in the summer, but wind-blown and snow-bound in the winter. Virginia was a state of contrasts. Washington, at its easternmost limit, was a tangle of concrete suburbs and malls—racially and ethnically diverse, busy, nearly a million people in the metropolitan area. The rural parts of the state, however—the areas around Catawba, for example—were quite different. They were agricultural. They'd voted heavily for Bob Dole in the 1996 election; the area near the trail was dotted with tobacco and soybean farms, and industrial-sized commercial turkey factories.

Ginny took out a yellow highlighter and ran it over the county names: Orange, Greene, Albemarle, Nelson, Amherst, Rockbridge, Rockingham, Augusta. She repeated these words again and again, quietly, tracing over the page with her fingertips. She imagined the words as a magical thing—names rising up off the map and filling the air around her with their sound. And then John was standing behind her in the doorway to the kitchen.

"What are you doing?" he asked.

"He's probably so cold," she said, turning to John. "It must be forty degrees out there tonight in the mountains."

"I can't believe Fielding lost his dog," John said.

"I can't believe it took this long."

John put his hand on her shoulder. "We'll find him," he said. "I know we will."

"How can you say that?" she asked.

"Easy," he answered. "Because I believe it."

But Virginia was still skeptical. The weather was a significant factor in Gonker's chances of survival. Winter was just beginning. She'd taken Gonker to the groomer a week before; now, his coat was short. It wouldn't protect him against the cold.

28

"In the Middle of the Night in a Dark House Somewhere in the World" is the title of the sixth and final episode of Swedish director Ingmar Bergman's TV miniseries *Scenes from a Marriage*. It is also a phrase that's evocative of a space we often occupy—solitary, away from daily life, in a private room, in quietude—in a dark house that is, in some way, our own.

Fielding returned that night to the apartment he was renting in West Falls Church. In the parking lot, walking among what felt like a hundred identical silver bullet-shaped sedans, he paused to let a woman with a stroller walk by him. She had a heavy-looking diaper bag over one arm, and on the other the leash of a little white dog— some kind of mutt—a dog, like Gonker, of somewhat uncertain lineage. She smiled at him as she passed, and Fielding caught a glimpse of her tiny, black-haired infant, sleeping in the stroller, peaceful. A shock moved through him then, a kind of clarity. Our potential lives, he suddenly saw, surround us each day.

Inside the apartment, though, everything felt foreign

and strange. Without Gonker, the place somehow felt barely inhabited. When Fielding walked through the door, he simply sat down in silence on his couch. He began paying attention to his breath. He was empty. The lack of food had hollowed him out and remade him. He was new. Though he still had a body, some essential part of him felt weightless.

One loss mirrors another loss mirrors another loss. And so, in this moment—this night in a dark house somewhere in the world—he began to think of Rebecca. Rebecca, who'd disappeared from his life so completely, those many years before. He started calling friends— channeling some sudden, implacable determination— and after an hour, he had it: her current phone number.

He looked down at the piece of paper, touched his fingertips to its smooth, cool surface. Rebecca had moved to a new city and started her life over without him. He picked up the telephone. One by one, he dialed the digits, pausing on the last one and looking, without really seeing anything, toward the window as he did. Finally, he did it. His finger pressed the final key.

Ringing. And then—quickly, much more quickly than he'd anticipated—there was Rebecca's voice. "Hello?" she said. And then, after a moment's silence: "Hello? Anyone there?"

Fielding felt an almost physical weight settle over him and saturate him. It was built of memories, fragments of memories: the sight of Gonker bounding off along the trail, the sight of the little girl in her incubator struggling to get her heart working. This heaviness stopped him; it physically arrested his voice. He realized that he wasn't going to say anything. He realized why he'd called. And so he waited there in silence. She said hello a few more times, then hung up. After a moment, the dial tone surged into his ear.

I'm sorry, Fielding thought. "Goodbye," he said aloud.

29

"The Appalachian Trail leads not merely north and south," wrote Harold Allen in 1934, "but upward to the body, mind, and soul of man."

In 1900, the trail's first great visionary, Benton MacKaye, graduated from Harvard University. After his graduation, MacKaye took a celebratory six-week hike, following a series of trails maintained with varying degrees of stewardship, relying on hand-drawn maps that he'd procured from numerous sources. Standing atop Stratton Mountain (which, today, is a ski resort and twenty-seven-hole championship golf course), MacKaye had a vision of a single, long trail connecting New England and the South, cutting through the peaks and valleys of America's Eastern Seaboard. He saw a place that would offer, as the plaque on Springer Mountain in Georgia now says, "a footpath for those who seek fellowship with the wilderness." It would take thirty-seven years for MacKaye's vision to become reality.

Any number of corporations would be overjoyed to develop the land that lies beneath the trail; it's rich in minerals, in coal, in natural gas. And yet the idea of the Appalachian Trail has, over the last century, trumped any potential industrial development. This is in part because of the grandeur of its open spaces; the scent of weather—rain, for example—gathering thick in the air, gathering on one side of a hill or a mountain, and then sweeping down toward you; rain on your skin; leaves rustling with each step, the feeling of mud on hands, on boots, underfoot; leaves changing color, leaves falling, snow on skeletal trees.

Bill Bryson concludes *A Walk in the Woods*—his hilarious first-person account of trying, and failing, to walk the Appalachian Trail—like this:

> I understand now, in a way I never did before, the colossal scale of the world. I found patience and fortitude that I didn't know I had. I discovered an America that millions of people scarcely know exists. I made a friend. I came home.

I came home.

Two hundred sixty-five mountains; 255 shelters, all of them drafty and wood-floored; twenty-two hundred miles of packed dirt and gravel path, crossing fourteen states; thousands of species of plants and animals. A series of waypoints with colorful, unusual names: Peaks of Otter, Blackhorse Gap, Rockfish Gap, the Priest.

And one lonely golden retriever.

30

MONDAY, OCTOBER 12, 1998

Day One of Search

Command Central.

A telephone—a cordless Panasonic—sitting on top of a hundred-year-old Knickerbocker icebox. A fax machine nearby. A computer just around the corner. Next to the microwave and the plastic immersion blender—shelves and shelves of antiques. HERCO MILD AND MELLOW: THE WORLD'S BEST 5-CENT CIGARS. Turn-of-the-century tin buckets hung from the wooden beams in the kitchen ceiling, buckets that had once contained RUTLAND'S SWEEPING COMPOUND or SWIFT'S SELECTED PORK BRAINS. Reed baskets—many of them made in the nineteenth century—clustered in every corner. The primary decorative theme was Americana. Intricately arranged, scrupulously dusted, overflowing.

In this environment, Ginny got started. She'd procured

stacks of phone books, too, from the public library. She had a Cuisinart coffeemaker always brewing a pot of coffee. And then the map of Virginia, spread out in front of her, and pens and pencils and highlighters, and a list of ideas. Leads. There was never, in Ginny's mind, any question about whether or not she'd try to find this dog—whether or not she'd push herself to her limits to do it, investing hours and hours of her time.

The important question was: Where to call first?

Animal hospitals, she decided.

They would be the most likely source of information. Then she'd try all the pounds, the animal-control facilities in the small towns on the wooded slopes of the vast Appalachian Mountains where Gonker had disappeared. Then the police in each municipality. And of course churches. And grade schools. And libraries. Then she would call every newspaper and send them faxes. And then charitable organizations—the Elks Lodge, the Rotary Club, the VFW. Then ranger stations. And city halls.

And that would only be the beginning.

She also planned on calling any businesses that might have a central place in the communities that she was scouring from here, from a distance: any general store, of course, and the Blue Ridge Parkway Authority, and local credit unions, and then radio stations, and newspapers, and TV stations—whose news anchors would be listed in local phone books and possibly eligible for a call at home. Then, of course, she'd set in on the secondary leads—

anyone recommended by the first set of calls. And then the tertiary leads.

As she made contacts, she'd keep every conversation sorted in a color-coded file folder. She'd started a countdown on a bright-orange pack of oversized Post-it Notes. She'd numbered each sheet—nineteen to zero—representing how many days they had until the fludrocortisone acetate and cortisol ran out. These were the synthetic hormones that kept Gonker alive; once they left his bloodstream, hope would be truly lost.

To make matters worse, it was early autumn, the beginning of the hunting season. Gonker, moving through the leaves, could easily be mistaken for something else, for a larger animal—a blur of motion, a deer darting for cover. Ginny imagined him shot by hunters. She imagined him wounded and staggering through the forest, collapsing on the cold ground, blood coursing out of him. Or she imagined him sick, and stumbling from his illness, wandering into some small town and being mistaken for a rabid dog—like the rabid dog in *To Kill a Mockingbird,* one of Virginia's beloved childhood books.

There were also coyotes. To a pack of coyotes, Gonker would be an ideal snack—soft and chewy and pleasantly dog-flavored. Ginny imagined her friend, eager to play with his wild cousins, walking right up to them, smiling—curious as to why they, too, were lost out here on the Appalachian Trail. They'd devour him in moments; he'd barely even have a chance to say hello.

There are hundreds of stories in every popular culture about dogs, especially about dogs and their heroic, unwavering faithfulness to human beings. Every country, it seems, has some kind of famous, legendary canine. Hachiko in Japan, of course. In Cádiz, Spain, a plaque honors Canelo, a dog whose owner died during dialysis at a local hospital; Canelo waited outside of that hospital for twelve years, hoping that his owner would once again walk through the revolving doors and take him home. In Argentina, for the past nine years, Capitán, a German shepherd, has been watching over his master's grave, refusing to leave—even in the most inclement weather. In Tolyatti, Russia, a bronze statue called *The Monument to Devotion* honors Constantine, the dog who returned, every day for seven years, to the intersection where his family were all killed in a car accident.

American culture also has famous stories of dogs traveling long distances to find their departed owners. Bobbie the Wonder Dog, for example, became famous for traveling twenty-five hundred miles to return to his family in Silverton, Oregon. This devotion is perhaps more poignant in the twentieth and twenty-first centuries, when humanity's worst aspects have been on such ample display. The mechanized slaughter of modern warfare, the incineration of hundreds of thousands of people with a single bomb, ethnic cleansing and tribal warfare in every part of the globe, the horrors of genocide—all of these are part of our current sense of ourselves, of our belief in the limits of what people will and will not do. But dogs are almost always decent—unchanging, unaltered, predictable. And their attitude toward us is unquestioningly kind. Dogs can make us more human—or more like what we imagine a good human to be. If we listen.

Maybe this is why their loss is so heartbreaking. We're skewered by the lost-animal fliers stapled to telephone poles, by the pleading posts across all forms of social media, begging for news of a missing companion. And it's not just dogs. Here's the photograph of Charlie, the beloved family cat, yawning into the camera, fat and fluffy. Here's Brantley, the eleven-pound lop-eared rabbit, his picture taken just before he disappeared in the middle of the night, digging his way underneath the fence in the backyard, uprooting the damask rose. Their loss implies the loss of the kind of innocence that doesn't exist very often in our contemporary world.

In a 1988 study for the *Journal of Mental Health Counseling,* the (aptly named) S. B. and R. T. Barker found that many dog owners actually voluntarily admitted feeling closer to their pets than to their families. In "The Human-Canine Bond: Closer Than Family Ties," Barker and Barker asked their test subjects to place icons representing their family members and pets in a circle, with the center of the circle representing themselves. The subjects were then told that the purpose of the test was to determine how close they felt to each being in their lives. The conclusions were dramatic. "A statistically significant difference was found between the self-canine distance and self–average family member distance," the researchers wrote, "with the dog closer to self than the average family member." The startling takeaway message? The dog was "placed closer to the self than any humans in 38% of the diagrams." Dogs, it seems, burrow into the deepest parts of ourselves. They live inside of us, in a part of the soul that we don't normally access. No matter what interior compartments we build, they transgress those boundaries. When they enter our lives, there is no clear way for us—*Homo sapiens sapiens* and *Canis lupus familiaris*—to pull back apart.

Ginny's handwriting in the faxes she sent across the state of Virginia expressed panic. This much is clear: the words were uneven and the letters didn't come neatly together. She was writing quickly, provisionally, sending notes to her growing list of contacts. But something else seems to live in those letters. In their stems and flourishes, there seemed to be a wistful hope. And she was begging—pleading, really—for help. Any kind of help. This is my beloved animal, her handwriting seems to say. Won't you help me find him? Won't you, kind stranger, help bring him back to me?

31

Day Two of Search
———————————
Eighteen Days Left

It's perfect, Fielding thought.

He'd designed a flier, sitting at his desk overnight, unable to sleep. Have you seen me? he typed, just above an image of Gonker looking mournfully up at the camera. The sky got lighter and lighter as he worked. He printed a hundred copies and put them in a stack by the door.

Despite his parents' objections, he'd already called and taken a week off from work. Fielding realized that he was no use in D.C.; all he did was pace his apartment, anyway, just waiting and waiting for the phone to ring. He called his mom as soon as the sun was up.

"I'm leaving for the trail," he said. "I'm going right now."

Ginny covered the phone with her hand. "He wants to

go back," she said to John. They were lying in bed. "He's going right now."

"Hell," John said, "I'll go with him. The way he's coming apart, I don't want him out there alone."

And so they set out, taking John's dark-green Ford Expedition and heading into the Appalachians, passing from the coastal lowlands of the capital region to the foothills of the mountain range, and then into the mountains themselves. They took Uli. The idea was to use Uli's scent to lure Gonker out of the woods. Gonker would smell his old friend and—with thoughts of home (and doughnuts) surging through his canine brain—come dashing out to greet him. Uli seemed excited about the forthcoming road trip. He was ready for adventure. He looked cheerfully through the back window, his tongue hanging out of the side of his mouth. Then he licked the glass. Then he barked at his reflection.

It was a long drive. They took Interstate 66 West for almost eighty miles, then got on Interstate 81 South. John saw the drive as an opportunity. He began a discussion of FDR's land-use policies, and the way the government had seized the property of farmers throughout the valley.

"FDR said that they had eminent domain," he told Fielding. "And he took them off the orchards. And that's what we're traveling through now. It's the mystical Appalachian countryside. The foundations of the old homesteads are decaying in the bushes. The ghosts—lost and never found."

"Hopefully, one of those ghosts isn't Gonker," Fielding said.

In the area north of Harrisonburg, right inside of the border of Rockingham County, they stopped for gas at a local convenience store. Immediately upon climbing out of the car, Fielding felt like he'd entered a different country. The speakers on the pump were playing at a deafening volume "There's Your Trouble" by the Dixie Chicks. Across the fuel bay from the Marshalls' Ford was a mud-covered Chevy pickup on giant Interco Super Swamper tires. The tires alone, Fielding noted, were almost as tall as he was. On the truck's gas tank was a stencil of Calvin, the mischievous boy from the *Calvin and Hobbes* comic books, peeing on the UVA logo.

"Typical grad student," John said as he got out of the car and started the pump.

Fielding went into the little mini-mart and located the bulletin board. He recycled some of the tacks from the other posters to hang his own, putting up three fliers, so that the picture of Gonker clearly dominated everything else on the board. When he turned around, he turned directly into the long white beard of an old man who'd somehow crept silently up behind him.

"The question is," the stranger said, "have you seen *him*?"

"I'm sorry?"

"I said, 'Have you seen *him*?' " He pointed to the ceiling.

"The roofer?" Fielding said.

The old man shook his head. "Jesus Christ—Him with a capital 'H'—your Lord and Savior."

The two men had a long—and polite—conversation. The evangelist's name was Dan Chambers, and he promised to pray for Fielding, his father, and the missing dog.

"Thank you, sir," Fielding said, accepting the offer—no matter the terms.

Before he left, though, Dan Chambers clutched Fielding's hand and held it tight. "Dear God," he said, "we prayin' for this young man and his whole family."

When Fielding settled into the passenger's side of the vehicle and arranged the remaining fliers neatly on his lap, he looked over at John. "I think I was just converted," he said.

Rural Virginia is one of the most beautiful places on earth, especially in mid-October. The leaves blazed in the last stages of their color, turning from a bright yellow to a deep ocher, from a fiery orange to a fading brown. Apple season. Foliage crunching underfoot. Wood smoke in the air. Every few miles, there were signs that led you to an orchard—to pick your own apples, or to buy fresh-pressed cider, or to watch the making of applesauce, something that almost every orchard did in big metal cauldrons.

Fielding thought a lot, as they were driving, about what the trip meant to him, and his dad. At one point, with the radio low and the defroster struggling to keep the

windows clear of condensation, Fielding glanced quickly
across the front-seat console.

"I want to say thanks, Dad," he said.

"We haven't accomplished anything," John said. "Caesar didn't thank his generals until they won."

"I'm not Caesar," Fielding said.

"Doesn't mean you can't act like him," John said.
"Everyone needs role models."

Small-town Virginia gave way to open country. The milepost where Fielding had lost Gonker was in the middle of
the wilderness, with a little gravel parking lot next to a
log-cabin lean-to, and a vast tract of open forestland. John
and Fielding took the Appalachian Trail north and south,
shouting for Gonker. They encountered tourists—on
the trail for the fall foliage—and hard-core thru-hikers,
heading south, mostly, racing winter. Almost everyone
was startled by the dog's unusual name.

"What's a Gonker?" one hiker asked.

Fielding handed her a flier.

For the people they encountered, they unquestionably
presented an unusual sight. Here was a white-haired older
gentleman, dressed in a wardrobe best described as business casual—loafers, pleated Dockers, and, as a flour-
ish, a Tyrolean fedora, forest-green and accented with a
feather. And Fielding, wearing a moth-eaten sweater and
torn Levi's, following close behind.

John had, at the last moment, decided to take his old

megaphone, a sacred family relic—the one from his days of playing six-man football for St. Stephen's Episcopal School in Alexandria, Virginia. Now he bellowed Gonker's name into it, the noise loud enough to be heard deep into the Appalachian woods. If Gonker *was* anywhere nearby, he would undoubtedly come running. What the hikers must have thought of these two strangely matched men—shouting a strange, made-up word as loudly as possible—no one will ever know.

They had no luck. Even though it was beautiful, the air was becoming cold, and after hours of yelling, and walking, and yelling, and walking, their feet and hands were numb. Fielding shivered as he walked—but still he refused to give up hope that, with the next yell, Gonker would come bounding out of the scrub brush.

"It's almost sunset," John finally said.

"We should keep going," Fielding said. "He could be moving at night, to stay safer."

"Dogs aren't nocturnal," John said. "Gonker especially. If he's anywhere now, he's napping."

For hours, they put the fliers on telephone poles across the county. And then—exhausted—they went to the drive-through at McDonald's. The sky had clouded over. It had begun to rain. Fielding and John sat in the car, eating their dinner out of grease-stained white paper bags. Uli nuzzled his way between the two front seats. They'd ordered him his favorite—a Big Mac—and he chewed on this contentedly, almost ruminatively. The radio played a country-and-western song about heartbreak.

Fielding stared out the window. This was truly miserable weather—forty degrees and a saturating dampness. It had started to rain harder. Poor Gonker, Fielding thought, out in this somewhere, soaked. In his mind, all he could see was the orange Post-it Note calendar on the wall in his parents' house. He'd taken to calling it, with gallows humor, "The Addison's Doomsday Countdown." Tomorrow there'd be one less day.

Fielding had made a reservation for that night at the only motel close to the trail, so that he and John could wake up early in the morning and get a couple more hours in as the sun rose. Now they drove to the little motel and pulled into its ten-space parking lot. Fielding ran inside to give the clerk his credit card. After a few minutes, he reappeared. He opened the passenger-side door and leaned inside, brushing the rain off his forehead. He looked at John and frowned.

"No dogs allowed," he said.

John nodded. "I expected no less," he said. "Get in," he added, and cranked the heater.

Fielding climbed inside. They sat for a moment in silence.

"We'll never find another place tonight," John finally said.

"We could sleep in the car," Fielding offered.

John shook his head. "I'll go take a look."

Fielding watched his father, Alpine hat and all, disappear inside the building. Five minutes passed, then five more. Finally, John came walking quickly back toward the SUV, a wide smile on his face. Without saying anything, he popped the trunk and took out his little rolling suitcase. Only then did he open the car door again and look at his son.

"Little laws," John said, gesturing toward the motel entrance and pausing for dramatic effect, "are for little men." Then he laughed—a loud, ebullient sound—contagious in its volume and rapidity. Before Fielding knew it, he was following John toward the doorway, Uli's leash in his hand.

"Dad," he said, "there's a three-hundred-dollar fine for pets."

John stopped and turned and nodded as he leaned closer to his son.

"Let me tell you a story, Fields," he said. "This is, I believe, an opportune moment." He reached out and took the end of Uli's leash. Much to the dog's bewilderment, John began using the leash as a prop, gesturing with its free end, pulling Uli back and forth as he talked.

"The ancient trading caravans on the Silk Road," John began, "would stop at campgrounds on their way to the Orient. And what—what do you think these campgrounds were called?"

Fielding stared at his dad. "Holiday Inns," he said.

"*Caravansaries!*" John exclaimed. "In a *caravansary,*

you see, there was a main entry point—with a guard, and places to rest behind it. You could bring your camels in past the guard, and they'd be safe."

"I don't think camels are allowed here, either," Fielding said. "And, Dad—why does this matter, anyway?"

"Well, my son," John said, "it matters because that's what we've got here. A *caravansary*. And so we have a duty, *an absolute duty,* to bring our camel in." Here he gestured to Uli, who barked. "We need to rest our camel in our room." John nodded. "Besides," he said, "the desk is so high that the clerk won't see the dog walk past."

"I'm not paying the fine," Fielding said.

John ignored this. "We need to rest our camel!" he shouted, throwing his arms in the air, a gesture of exuberance. And he turned toward the building and, lifting his feathered hat high in the air, walked inexorably forward. He didn't look back.

What choice did Fielding have? He simply followed along, pulling the wheeled suitcase, his mind wandering to long-ago spice traders who sat atop camels on bejeweled blankets, who walked through the desert for thousands of miles, traveling invisible roads, navigating by the stars, by the light of the distant, unblinking, luminous moon.

32

WEDNESDAY, OCTOBER 14, 1998

Day Three of Search
_____
Seventeen Days Left

And they did not, in fact, get caught—father, son, and dog. The motel did not discover them. John's plan worked just as he'd imagined. They sneaked Uli in and out, and spent the next day on the trail, heading south this time, then looping back north.

As they walked, Fielding's stomach pain—exacerbated by the anxiety, perhaps—grew worse and worse. The only thing that worked, when it got this bad, was not eating at all. And so that's what he did all day: he denied himself food. And in this denial there was a simplicity, an ease. All these difficult questions—what to eat, when to eat it, how much of it to eat—disappeared. There was just emptiness. And in that emptiness, no pain.

They passed a half-dozen orchards that day, stopping

at each to hand out fliers and examine the bubbling metal cauldrons of applesauce, the century-old juice presses, the fruit-heavy apple trees. John sampled a great deal of applesauce as they talked to everyone about their missing dog—and Fielding tried to seem as if he was eating, too. He'd manage a few mouthfuls, and immediately it felt as if they were burning their way through his gut. When his dad wasn't looking, he'd empty his dish into the fire. And so the day continued. Fielding and John sought out the advice, especially, of the trail's thru-hikers. They were, after all, the ones covering the greatest distance.

Standing near those kettles, in the orchards, with the smell of freshly made applesauce floating through the air, John and Fielding shared their story again and again. They encountered tourists—Germans, mostly—who were in Virginia for the end of the autumn foliage. They encountered more hikers—men and women with neoprene pouches of water on their backs, and big metal-frame packs that extended several feet above their heads. They encountered one woman—Sally Kramer, the owner of a local drugstore—who took half a dozen fliers and promised to saturate her town, Fulks Run, with them.

"I'll put 'em up at both stores in town, and the church, and the VFW," she said. "And that'll do it."

There were hunters, too—all wearing some shade of electric orange. They'd come in from their stands periodically and join the tourists at the applesauce cauldrons. Fielding had never seen so much Day-Glo clothing. From a distance, they looked like tiny fires.

Though Fielding had perhaps imagined that he would have nothing in common with anyone gathered around these fires, the opposite was true. "I'm looking for my dog," Fielding said to one man—a big, gruff-looking hunter who wore an orange safety vest and an M.R. Ducks mesh baseball cap. "I took him off-leash and he bolted into the woods."

The man was quiet for a while. He'd been chewing Kodiak smokeless tobacco, the Premium Wintergreen flavor. Now he spat into the dirt.

"When I was a little boy," he told Fielding, his face emptying of affect, "I lost my grandma's poodle."

Fielding nodded. He could smell the minty scent of the Kodiak. He looked around at the twisted, nearly naked trees, their gold and orange leaves scattered across the ground in a shiny mosaic.

"Did you find him?" Fielding asked.

The man shook his head. "I cried like a baby." He spat again. "That poodle was damn near a genius. But when he got off-leash. Boom. Gone. Just like that."

For Ginny, day three was a blur of faxes and letters and phone calls. Her tone, in these communications, was doleful and distressed:

Attn: Tina
Nelson County Times
(804) 946-2684

We are desperately looking for a lost family pet—the
attached gives you the details—we thought an ad in
your paper could bring good results—I am also sending
a photo—I don't think you can use it but you can tell
what a sweet doggie our Gonker is—
Thank you for your help—Ginny Marshall
Fields' Mom (owner's mom)

The letter reads in a breathless way. There are no peri-
ods. There's no punctuation, at all, other than the dashes,
which aren't quite grammatically correct. These dashes
seem to reflect, instead, a kind of momentary pause,
the wild-eyed look of a soldier surveying the battlefield
from an elevated position and seeing danger at every turn.

You can tell, Ginny writes, *what a sweet doggie our
Gonker is.* Can you, though? The photograph is simply a
photograph of a golden retriever. Good-natured, sure, but
perhaps little more than that. The picture is even a little
blurry. But Ginny's love—the love that's spilling out of
these letters—is the thing that's most evident.

Wintergreen Police
Officer Graves
(804) 325-1464

Thank you for your guidance—attached is the information on our Dear Lost Dog Gonker we are desperate to Find him—Could you please post the information wherever you think it might be seen.

In the notes to herself as well, Ginny has the same style, as if she is considering idea after idea, trying to get any sense of how to approach the problem. *"Will need flashlight,"* she scrawls on one piece of notebook paper, *"to catch the shine of his eyes—that's how dad and I spotted him out back one night when he didn't want to come in."* Another unfinished—interrupted—note reads: *"Just got first call. Near Maupin Field Shelter, near Reed's Gap—SEEN—a dog like Gonker. But—many miles north of—"* The writing trails off the page.

It was difficult, having the patience for the fax machine. The outgoing signal would be received, and the machine would whine—a noise that Ginny came to dread almost as much as the busy signal, or the line that rang and rang without answer. Her machine—a Magnafax Telecopier—was nearly twenty years old. It transmitted and received with glacial slowness, its transfer rate slower, she sometimes complained, than hand-delivering a document.

So she endured. Fax after fax whined out into the atmosphere. And then—finally—the transmission that would change everything.

It was a version of her standard letter. This time, though, it was addressed to Bill Kirby, an editor at *The News Virginian,* a small paper in the heart of Appalachian country. Ginny sent off the fax and then turned to the next one. As was the case with many of her other letters, there was no response. But then, after an hour or so, the phone rang.

The News Virginian isn't a huge newspaper. It has certainly felt the effects of the decline of print journalism. Its advertising revenues declined—steadily—throughout the first decade and a half of the new century. Its circulation, as of 2015, was just under seven thousand.

In 1998, its newsroom was the size of a church basement, and held a few partially disassembled copiers and an offset printing machine that was perpetually in the process of being repaired. At one corner of the room was a recycling bin with a miniature basketball hoop above it; reporters would crumple their drafts and throw them through the net. The bin was overflowing. This was, however, part of the romance of the room, along with the lingering scent of cigarette smoke, which—no matter how long the business stayed smoke-free—seemed to be deep within the very grain of the walls.

The thing that had kept *The News Virginian* running, over the decades, was its devotion to the community, to the municipality of Waynesboro, Virginia—including all of its human-interest stories, its high-school sports, its regional elections, its city-council debates. Waynesboro wasn't large—roughly twenty thousand people—but it did have a deep sense of civic pride. Named after General "Mad" Anthony Wayne—the Revolutionary War general who earned his nickname by leading a group of 1,350 soldiers on a nighttime bayonet-only mountainside raid of British positions in the Battle of Stony Point—Waynesboro has always attracted an independent-minded kind of individual, and the local paper was the broadest, most public form of communication in town. It was Waynesboro's hub—in a way that the national or even the Charlottesville papers just couldn't be.

When Ginny's fax came in, it was one of many—but perhaps the only one that was handwritten in pencil. And the story immediately caught Kirby's attention: the innocent love of the lost pet, the prospect of the looming death. He walked back to his desk, picked up the phone, and dialed the number on the fax; it had a 703 area code, so it could only be from a small section of the state, the suburbs of Washington, D.C.

The phone rang only once before Ginny answered.

"Marshall residence," she said.

Breathless. As if she were perched over the receiver, waiting for that ring. Which—of course—she was. Kirby introduced himself and thanked her for sending him the letter.

Ginny, for her part, was astonished. This was, after days and days, her first real break. Within seconds the whole story came pouring out—including Oji, the Akita, and some details from her childhood. Kirby listened. He took notes. Finally, he said, "Can you get us a picture of the dog? We'd need it by seven p.m. You could send it by e-mail."

There was a pause in the conversation.

"What's e-mail?" Ginny asked, her voice light and inquisitive.

Kirby sighed.

"Never mind," he said. "We'll figure out another way."

But it was already three-thirty. By five-thirty, Ginny had gotten in touch with Fielding at the motel. He explained e-mail to her but wasn't able to help any further. He couldn't drive down to McLean from where they were and then drive back; that would take at least six hours. Kinko's might work, he suggested—but he didn't know if the file was too big to send. It was, after all, an entire photograph. In color.

She would have to take the image to Waynesboro herself, Fielding said—drive it there and deliver it by hand. That was the only way it would get there by Kirby's deadline. Ginny accepted this. Fielding would have to talk her through the process of taking it off of the computer and putting it onto a floppy disk. "It's not that hard," Fielding said. "I promise."

But just then Virginia had an idea. "I'll call you right back," she said.

Across the street, on a grassy slope, lived the Elmores. A devout Mormon family, they had ten children. As Mormons, they were bound by their code of ethics to say yes whenever someone asked them for help of any kind. Ginny asked the Elmore boys, each spring and autumn, to rotate the rugs in her living room—to bring them out onto the front steps and beat the dust out of them, carry them to the basement, bring the fall rugs up, and lay them out. And then she'd give them each a glass of chocolate milk and Oreos.

This would be, Ginny reflected, a perfect task for the oldest Elmore, who was eighteen and about to leave on his Mormon mission to Brazil. He understood all of these new things: floppy disks and image files. He could drive the picture up to Waynesboro. What would be more edifying for him, after all, than the opportunity to incur the blessings of the Lord through service? By helping a family—and a dog—in need?

33

From: *THE NEWS VIRGINIAN*
October 15, 1998

"Gonker" Missing on Appalachian Trail

A golden retriever mix who answers to the name of "Gonker" was lost Saturday, Oct. 10 on the Appalachian Trail. . . .

He was last seen near the Maupin Field Shelter near Reed's Gap. Gonker is a 6-year-old, neutered, male golden retriever mix. He is a golden color and has white on his paws, tummy, and chest. He was wearing a purple and white herringbone pattern dog collar with tags. He is current on all his shots.

Gonker looks quite healthy but is suffering from a serious illness. He has Addison's Disease—an adrenal gland disorder—for which he receives medication. He needs to see his vet again on Nov. 2 or he will deteriorate rapidly. His condition makes him stagger and fall. The owner does not want people to think he has rabies.

Stress aggravates his condition. He gets very upset whenever he is separated from his owner. The family is fearful that he is hungry, confused, and frightened.

Gonker is a very intelligent and loving dog. He responds well to his name. Under happier conditions, he loves to retrieve a stick or a ball.

The owner is "totally heartbroken." Gonker has been his constant companion for six years. A $500 reward is being offered for his safe return. Contact (703) xxx-xxxx with any information.

34

THURSDAY, OCTOBER 15, 1998

Day Four of Search
_____
Sixteen Days Left

Ginny was startled awake just before six-thirty by the persistent ringing of the telephone. Fielding and John were still on the road; she was alone in her king-sized bed, something that she found deeply disorienting. For more than thirty years, she'd slept with her foot touching John's leg each night. Without that contact, she found it difficult to go to sleep.

She struggled to find her reading glasses on the bedside table. "Hello?" she said, rubbing the bridge of her nose and straining to listen to the crackling of the phone line.

"I seen him," said the voice on the other end of the line. There was no preamble, no explanation—just an old woman with a thick Appalachian accent, and possibly a touch of booze for good measure. "I done seen him and it don't look good."

"I'm sorry, ma'am?" Ginny said. "Can you repeat that? Are you referring to our dog, Gonker?"

"My neighbor got him," the woman continued. Ginny kept listening as the woman took a deep swallow of whatever she was drinking. "He's a bad man."

After five minutes, Ginny had the whole story. This woman's neighbor, Claude, had animals—all *types* of animals—locked up in cages in his basement. There was no telling what sorts of things he did with them. And now Gonker was down there, for sure. She'd seen him lead a chubby golden retriever down the back stairs just this morning.

It was a strange story, but it was their first lead. Ginny thanked the woman, jotted down her address, and hung up the phone. In an hour, she decided, she'd send Fielding and John up to Charlottesville. They'd drive the thirty minutes to see Claude—who was a bad man. What else could they do? They had to follow up on every lead.

She put her head back down on the pillow. She thought again of Gonker, looking for her, for Fielding, for anyone from the family. Her heart ached—physically ached—in her chest. She closed her eyes for a moment, craving just a little more rest. The phone rang again.

"Hello?" Ginny said, more prepared this time, pad and pencil ready on the bedside table.

"I know where your dog is, Ms. Marshall. I swear I do."

It was a man's voice this time, but again heavy with an Appalachian accent.

Ginny shook her head and squinted at the paper. "What's your name, sir?" she said.

"My name ain't important. What matters is that your dog's in the highway, medium."

"The highway, medium?" Ginny said. "You mean the median? The highway median?"

"Exactly," the man said. "Right where the grass is. Right outside of town here, not far from where I live."

"Terrific," Ginny said. "This is great."

"He got hit by a car," the man said.

Ginny's breath caught in her throat. "Oh no," she said softly. "Oh God, please no—anything but that."

"They got the ambulance out there for him," the man continued, "but that don't matter none. They called the priest, too, from the Catholic church." Ginny frowned out through the darkness. She put the pen down.

"I have to say, sir," she said, "that seems unlikely."

"And they're fixin' to call the governor."

Silence.

"Maybe the governor can get him a reprieve? He's not hurting anyone, you know. He's just a dog, after all. Right?"

"Yes, sir," Ginny said. "Thank you for calling."

"No problem, ma'am. I'm just an alert American citizen, ready and willing to help."

In retrospect, Ginny conceded that publishing her home telephone number in the newspaper was, at the very least, an adventurous decision.

The next call came fifteen minutes later. Ginny had

managed to make it downstairs and brew a pot of coffee. "Have you found your dog?" a man's voice asked when she answered, harsh and petulant and aggressive.

"Not yet," Virginia said.

"Well, you ain't going to, neither," the caller told her. And then he hung up the phone.

Ginny was suddenly viewing—without filter—the breadth of response that her vulnerability could attract. Over the next few days she would witness so many people who were angry at weakness. Powerless themselves, unable to build the kind of life they wanted, for one reason or another, they abused her. She was convenient. She was accessible now. This was something she'd seen every day at the Women's Center. And she'd lived it, too, as a little girl.

Later that afternoon, Fielding and John pulled up to the house in Charlottesville. It was raining as they parked on the street in the residential neighborhood near the university. In the distance, a police siren rose and then fell, rose and then fell, a steady pulse of warning.

"I'll keep the engine running," John said. "You check it out, Fields."

"He's probably a murderer."

"Nonsense, son. You have an overactive imagination."

"Then why are you staying in the car?"

John began laughing. He kept laughing—and laughing—and laughing—until tears came from the corners of his eyes. "Because," he finally managed, "someone needs to drive the getaway vehicle."

Of course, Claude turned out not to be a bad man. Quite the contrary. He was rescuing animals—rescuing and rehabilitating them and releasing them into the wild. He worked in partnership with the university and the local humane society. What Claude did have, however, was an ongoing feud with his neighbor, who'd never forgiven him for building an ugly fence in their backyard— more than two decades before.

In New York City, however—behind the Brutalist concrete-and-glass façade of 450 West Thirty-third Street, the Associated Press global headquarters—an editor at a regional desk was looking at the morning's stories. And there, among all the other news, was that picture of Gonker. She paused. As she looked at the golden retriever, for just a moment, her breath caught in her throat. Here was a little story, a story about a lost dog, barely bigger than two hundred words. But it seemed, somehow, to have a bigger, deeper resonance. It could be of interest to the broader public.

She decided to send it out over the wire.

How far can a single word travel—especially if you yourself make it up while enveloped in a haze of suspiciously odorous smoke? In the case of Fielding's self-invented name for his dog, the answer is: to 1,700 newspapers and 5,100 television and radio outlets in over 115 countries. On any given day, half of the globe's population will see news from an Associated Press story. This was the scope of Gonker's journey—begun in that decrepit, mildewed shack on the outskirts of Charlottesville, Virginia. Reporters in Russia, in China, in Egypt, in Burkina Faso, in New Zealand, in Chile—they all looked down at that feed and saw the story come in across the wire. How many of them read it? Thousands, certainly. Uncountable numbers of people looked down and pondered, for at least a moment, the poor dog's name.

35

Day Five of Search

Fifteen Days Left

"I am standing here in front of the Exxon in Charlottesville, at a pay phone," said the voice on the other end of the line.

"And you called me just to let me know, sweetheart," Ginny said. "How nice."

"I'm having corn dogs for breakfast," John said. "And they're delicious."

"That's great," Ginny said. "But I'm going back to sleep."

"No, wait," John said. "There's more. What do you think I'm looking at?" When Ginny didn't say anything, John continued. "There's the corn dog, certainly," he said, "but there's also a copy of the Charlottesville *Daily Progress*."

"The local paper?"

"The local paper. And guess whose name I'm looking at, right here on the front page?"

Ginny sat up in bed.

"Gonker?" she said.

"We've been busy," John said. "We've been talking to a few people, too." And then John read her the entire article, aloud.

From: *THE DAILY PROGRESS*
Charlottesville, Virginia

Wandering pooch has pal worried

CHARLOTTESVILLE—He's lost, scared, in need of medication, probably sick and possibly dying.

Fields Marshall's best friend is alone in the woods along the Appalachian Trail and there's little Mr. Marshall can do.

"I've contacted everyone I can think of," said Mr. Marshall, his low, quiet voice sad but under control. "I've put fliers up all around. I've gone looking for him. I don't know what else to do."

Mr. Marshall's story is of a welcome mountain respite gone awry. It began October 10 when he and his friend Gonker, a 6-year-old golden retriever mix and Mr. Marshall's constant companion, took a hike to get away from the stress of the work week.

Along the way, Gonker bounded off the trail to smell the woods. He was last seen near Maupin Field Shelter wearing a purple and white herringbone pattern dog collar and tags with a microchip ID inserted between his shoulder blades. The shelter is near Reed's Gap— close to Milepost 16 on the Blue Ridge Parkway at the western edge of Nelson County, south of Afton.

Medication Needed

But this is no ordinary lost dog story. If Gonker isn't found soon, he may die. . . .

"Gonker has Addison's disease and it affects his adrenal glands, gets them out of balance," Mr. Marshall explained. "We discovered it when Gonker kept getting more and more tired and finally I couldn't get him to move. When I took him to the vet, he said he was near death. It took them some time to figure out why."

To keep his adrenal glands under control, Gonker receives regular medication. The medication keeps Gonker fetching sticks and chasing balls like any other golden retriever.

"We've got until about November 1 before he would normally need his shot, but if he's scared and stressed he's likely to get sick quicker and need medication," Mr. Marshall said.

"If he gets sick, the illness will make him start to stagger around. People could be scared that he's a sick dog, a rabid dog. He's sick, but he's not a danger. I don't want someone to mistake his disease for rabies and kill him," he said.

It may seem odd now, but when Gonker ran off the trail, Mr. Marshall didn't worry.

"I didn't think anything about it. When we lived in Charlottesville we walked the woods a lot and he'd wander away for 10, 15 or 20 minutes and always come right back," said Mr. Marshall, an independent computer programmer who lives in West Falls Church.

"Only this time, he didn't."

Loving companion

Mr. Marshall adopted Gonker from the Charlottesville-Albemarle Society for the Prevention of Cruelty to Animals when the dog was a puppy and Mr. Marshall a student at the University of Virginia.

"We do everything together. We spend a lot of time with each other. Now that I live in the city I try to do right by him by taking him out as often as I can," Mr. Marshall said.

"That's why I didn't really think too much about it until he'd been gone for about 30 minutes. I don't know if he chased a deer or just got on a scent and got turned around or what happened. All I know is I need to find him," Mr. Marshall said.

With fliers posted all along the trail and all the humane societies notified, there is little more for Mr. Marshall to do but wait.

"I'm hoping that somehow someone finds him and we can get him to the vet before it's too late," Mr. Marshall said sadly, his tears nearly audible. "When I adopted him I promised to take care of him until he got old. Now I just hope he doesn't die before he gets there."

Virginia marveled that it was a little different from what she herself thought about it—marveled that Gonker's story was transformed each time it came back to her, if only slightly. Tears filled Ginny's eyes.

"Oh, John," she said, "what do you think?"

"I think I love you, Ginny. And that this dog—what can I say?—he's magic."

"Do you really think that we'll find him?"

"We're marching on, General," John said. "We're marching on. Don't lose faith."

"Don't lose Fields," Ginny said.

"I've got him on a short leash," John said. "Don't worry. He's doing great."

36

SATURDAY, OCTOBER 17, 1998

Day Six of Search
―――――――――
Fourteen Days Left

All the while, though, the Addison's Doomsday Countdown was ticking.

Late at night on the 17th, Ginny's phone rang again— the sixth call that day. She almost didn't answer it. It had been a long day, and her voice was hoarse from talking on the phone. She'd had to explain Gonker's story so many times that it was starting to feel rehearsed; she was losing track of the emotional drive of it, its urgency. It was starting to come unmoored in time.

"Marshall residence," she said softly, holding the receiver in the crook of her palm and resting her head on her folded knuckles. "This is Ginny Marshall."

There was a pause on the other end of the line. Then, a wavering voice: "Ginny," a woman said, "this is Rosa Lee Chittum." Another pause. Ginny's eyes widened as she recognized the woman's name. "You may have read about my family in the news."

Babies are still—even in this age of technology and electronic tracking bracelets and exhaustive safety protocols—switched at birth. Some estimates indicate that it happens as many as three times per year in the United States. Chance is merciless; it has no regard for human beings, for the things we imagine for ourselves, the narratives we build around our lives. And a mistake—though small—can have vast consequences.

The story of Callie Johnson and Rebecca Chittum is an example of this kind of story. Somehow—in the early-morning hours of July 1, 1995, at the University of Virginia Medical Center in Charlottesville—a nurse lost track of the babies' identities. They were swapped and sent home with the wrong parents. For three years, both families reared the girls as their own.

But then, as the centerpiece of an elaborate paternity dispute involving Callie Johnson's father, a DNA test exposed the truth: not only was Callie Johnson *not* her father's child, but she was also not her mother's.

The Johnson family scrambled to put together how this was possible. A search of hospital records turned up Kevin and Whitney Chittum and their baby daughter, who was born at almost exactly the same time as Callie. More tests were conducted. The mistake was pinpointed, and then, on July 4, 1998, the day before the results of the last DNA test were confirmed, the story took a tragic turn.

As Kevin and Whitney drove to the state fair in Salem, Virginia, they tried to pass a tractor-trailer in the pouring rain. The road was slick, and their minivan spun out of control, fishtailing into the other lane of the highway, where a tanker truck flattened it. The two vehicles careened over a bridge and plunged a hundred feet through the air and onto another highway. Everyone died. Callie never got to meet her biological mother and father.

In the autumn of 1998, when Gonker went missing, this was still the main story of loss in the Virginia news. Funds were being set up for Callie's education, and the two families were struggling with how they might introduce Rebecca Chittum to her parents. The grandparents were distraught over the loss of their children as well—and the media spotlight didn't help things at all.

Ginny, for her part, couldn't get these families out of her mind, and she had considered writing a condolence letter to them, offering her support and prayers—anything she could give them. She spoke to several good friends about it. She and John discussed the tragedy often. They felt this was another example of the indifference of fate, of human events that were simply beyond the boundaries of rational understanding.

And so, that night, listening to Rosa Lee Chittum—Kevin's mother—introduce herself, Ginny was speechless. Should she tell Rosa Lee that she felt like her friend, that the Chittum family had been on her mind over these last three months? Or would that be unwelcome? An intrusion?

But then Rosa Lee Chittum shared her reason for calling. Like many others, she'd read about Gonker in *The News Virginian*. Sitting down for a cup of coffee in the early morning, she'd read the story and then, quite to her surprise, she'd realized that she was crying; tears were cascading across her cheeks and falling uncontrollably onto the newspaper.

It was, she told Ginny, the first time since her son had died—since the terrible crash on July 4—that she'd been able to cry. She'd been in shock that whole time, unable to gain access to the part of her that had to let go—unable to grieve. Somehow, Gonker's story had unlocked that for her. She'd spent the entire day in tears, but now, even though she was still a wreck, she felt a little better.

"I don't know what to say, ma'am." Ginny shook her head. "That's just the kind of dog Gonker is," she said. "He brings people together, somehow. I don't even know how."

"You find him, then," Rosa Lee said.

"We're doing our best, ma'am," Ginny said.

They hung up a few minutes later. Sitting there, astonished, encased by the echoing, spinning sound of the dial tone, Ginny felt suddenly shot through with luck. She felt guilty, too—it was a complicated feeling. She was grateful for John, for all of her family, who would support her in her times of crisis, even if they'd also helped create those crises. Fielding and John had rushed to Gonker's—and Ginny's—defense. They'd smuggled a dog into a motel; they'd spent the better part of a week rampaging up and down the Appalachian Trail with a megaphone. This was her new definition of family, then: the people who rush to your defense with a megaphone, in times of trouble.

Would her own father have done the same? After hanging up the phone with Rosa Lee Chittum, Ginny walked into the living room in a ruminative mood. The manic intensity of the last twenty-four hours had worn her out— the phone ringing again and again, the crank calls, the well-intentioned people, Rosa Lee Chittum.

Ginny turned the brass key in the base of the hearth to make the gas fireplace come to life. She'd poured her usual glass of wine with black-currant syrup. Now she sat on the sofa, her eyes moving between the soft-toned painting of lilies that hung above the fireplace, and the fire itself. The flames were steady and continuous, fed by the valve of natural gas. They did not waver. In this way, they were different from a wood-burning fire, which flared and died down, flared and died down. Ginny shook her head, overwhelmed by the simple memory of her father's face when he walked in the door on the day that Oji had died. His serious eyes. His frown. She could see him so clearly even these forty-five years later—his image etched with that indelible weight of childhood memory.

And then she knew what she had to do next. She stood up, almost knocking over the lamp in the process. She rushed to Command Central. There, in one corner, was a large roll of cork—replacement cork for the corkboard in the kitchen. She grabbed a pair of scissors and sliced off a long rectangle of the material. Next she picked up a roll of tape and taped the rectangle to the back of the front door of the house. Then she got a notecard and a Sharpie. She wrote:

TEAM OF HEROES

Then she pinned the notecard to the top of the long sepia strip. Now she took out a second card and wrote the name "Rosa Lee Chittum." In the corner of that card, she carefully inked—and circled—the number 1. Rosa Lee was her first hero. She pinned this card directly beneath the first. There was room on the board for about two dozen cards, she figured. And probably she'd need each and every one.

37

SUNDAY, OCTOBER 18, 1998

Day Seven of Search
_____
Thirteen Days Left

What is heroism?

Is the idea of it irrelevant, in some ways, to the majority of Americans, who lead lives that don't seem to call them to heroic action? Waking each day, driving a congested freeway to an office, sitting in a cubicle for ten hours—this doesn't seem like a pattern of living that could lead to heroism of any kind, certainly not in the cinematic sense of the word.

Wesley Autrey was a fifty-year-old construction worker waiting for the subway with his two young daughters on a cold morning in January 2007 in New York City. A few feet away from him, a young man, Cameron Hollopeter, began having a seizure. Hollopeter stumbled toward the tracks and fell onto them—just as the train was roaring into the station. Autrey didn't hesitate; he leapt onto the tracks and pressed himself over this complete stranger's body. Five cars of the train passed over them, clearing the two men by less than an inch; the bottom of the axle left smears of grease on Autrey's light-blue stocking cap. The train stopped. Onlookers were screaming; Autrey's daughters were weeping and calling for their father. Then his voice boomed out over the commotion: "Tell my daughters I'm okay. Tell them we're both okay." The screams changed into shouts of astonishment and then, spontaneously, applause.

Yet these moments are rare. Or are they, really? Not at all, argues Phil Zimbardo, the founder of the Heroic Imagination Project, an institute that wants to redefine heroism for the twenty-first century. A hero, in Zimbardo's eyes, is anyone who obeys the four following principles:

1. Voluntary action.
2. Action done in service of people or communities in need.
3. Action involving risk.
4. Action that doesn't require any material compensation.

"Heroism is not an abstract concept," Zimbardo argues, "but a lifestyle generated through continual personal choice."

This definition is interesting, but one of its pillars—risk—is a difficult thing to calculate. One of the most remarkable poems about heroism in the English language is Robert Hayden's "Those Winter Sundays." Though it has only fourteen lines, it carries the weight of an entire relationship inside of it, a relationship that is, at its essence, a heroic one. "Sundays too my father got up early / and put his clothes on in the blueblack cold . . ." The father makes the fire for his family each morning—despite the pain that debilitates his body. And—poignantly—no one thanks him.

Heroic work can be individual work, work performed against an adversary in the body itself: persistence through illness, through injury. In 1968, at the Olympic Games in Mexico City, fifty-seven runners finished the men's marathon. The last to cross the finish line was John Stephen Akhwari of Tanzania; he was one hour later than all the other competitors. Injured in the middle of the race—the ligaments of his knee torn during a fall—Akhwari had bandaged his leg and continued moving, both walking and jogging, his body clearly in agony as he went. He was limping severely as he came into Olympic Stadium. This was the moment he'd trained for—but altered, changed in a way that he could never have predicted.

By that time, most of the crowd had left. But those who had stayed, kept in place by the whispered news—*there's still a runner on the course*—stood and began to applaud. And they didn't stop—not as he staggered toward the finish line, not as he crossed it, not as he collapsed on the ground in pain, not for many minutes afterward. "My country did not send me five thousand miles to start the race," Akhwari said, when asked why he'd persevered. "They sent me five thousand miles to finish the race."

But heroism is possible in nearly any context. Certainly the burden of things-to-do at work can be, for many of us, an extreme one. This is hardly new to the age of e-mail; even though we sometimes feel that the avalanche in our in-box is a new development, it's not, not really. Work has always been time-consuming and difficult. What is conveyed now in e-mails came, in 1998, in letters and phone calls. The individuals who helped Ginny were all dealing with their own professional emergencies, their own office crises.

This is all by way of saying that any deviation from the norm, any going-out-of-your-way-to-do-something-for-a-stranger, has a certain amount of heroism attached to it in our contemporary society. Zimbardo falls short of saying the thing that many of us intuitively feel, here in early-twenty-first-century America: helping someone, anyone, in any way at all, is our overbusy culture's version of a heroic act. This is sad, sure. But to ignore the possibility that it's true is potentially to ignore a significant truth about the country in which we live. "Many social norms just don't make sense to people drowning in digital communication," writes Nick Bilton in the March 10, 2013, issue of *The New York Times*.

On October 18, Ginny got a call from Mary Kay at the Animal Hospital of Waynesboro. She'd heard Ginny's story and had sprung into action, getting together a list of all of the veterinary clinics in a hundred-mile radius. She faxed it to Ginny along with a kind note. The note filled Ginny with hope—with the sense that she might not be alone, searching for a dog from afar, isolated and insignificant. She went to the front door, notecard and pushpin in hand. Her list had now grown—and she'd added an underline.

TEAM OF HEROES

Rosa Lee Chittum
Bill Kirby and The News Virginian
Mary Kay

And later that night there were more. First there was Jenni at the Inn at Afton, who photocopied the phonebook pages for a variety of different types of businesses and faxed them to Ginny, along with notes about who might be most helpful. Then there was Laurie at Rodes Farm Stables, who hung dozens of fliers on Gonker's behalf, and called almost daily to keep Ginny posted about her own search. Then there was Connie Baber, a resident of Waynesboro, who wrote her own description of the situation and posted it at the Village Market in town. Connie then drove around to various veterinary offices on Ginny's behalf—on behalf of a total stranger—and quizzed the personnel about the lost dogs that had come through their offices over the past week. She told them that Gonker could possibly be identified by his microchip, something that was new technology in 1998.

And so, what had only been an idea this morning now seemed formidable fact. It was a team, without doubt. Ginny had a team in the field. It felt like a squadron, in fact, a phalanx—sweeping out in formation to cover the land.

38

MONDAY, OCTOBER 19, 1998

Day Eight of Search

Twelve Days Left

The smallest hours of the morning. Fielding was in a hotel room with his dad, who was sleeping contentedly, snoring, his stomach rising and falling with a regular rhythm.

Fielding, though, was fighting cramps. The raw, pulsing, gnawing pain in his gut. Pain like a meal—indigestible. Ropes of pain, turning him over on his mattress. Thick. He twisted his body in agony, trying to find a comfortable way to lie down, but there was none. He hunched his back. He stretched himself out flat, his thighs taut with tension, trying to keep himself straight on the mattress. He hunched in a fetal ball on the very bottom corner of his bed. Panicked, he tried to use his yoga breathing—muted, raspy—to calm the nausea. It didn't work.

And then he was in the bathroom. There was just no other choice. He locked the door and knelt in front of the toilet and reached into his throat. It didn't work at first, not immediately, and he had to move his fingers from right to left, almost tickling the smooth skin there, touching the back of his throat with his fingertips. Then there it was, the food rushing upward, triggered by the gag reflex, rocketing out of his stomach, filling the toilet bowl with what he'd eaten earlier that night. And he was gasping, and clutching at the porcelain with both hands. And the pain was gone; the ropes were dimming away, fading. With his mouth full of the foul taste of bile, he leaned against the stucco wall of the motel-room bathroom, breathless, panting, his body unruly, unmanageable, a vicious, hateful thing.

John was still asleep. What would he have done if he'd known about his son's suffering? When you are a parent, your children's physical bodies become—in a way—an extension of your own. You almost feel their illnesses yourself; when they suffer even minor accidents—skinned knees, bruised shins—you can't help flinching. In a way, Fielding was shielding his father from the pain of his condition. Though it was misguided, Fielding wanted to protect his father from the knowledge of it.

Uli, though, had more acute hearing. He could tell something was wrong with Fielding, and had followed him toward the bathroom. He lay down in front of its door. He put his nose to the gap at the threshold. He whined. He scraped at the wood with his paw, his nails clattering on the strip of metal across the doorjamb. Fielding supported himself on his hands and knees, cold sweat breaking out across his forehead and the planes of his cheeks. "It's okay, boy," he whispered. "Don't worry, Uli. I'll be right there."

Eventually that night, Fielding managed to get his body to rest. He collapsed on the bed across from John and, soothed by his father's steady breathing, fell into a shallow, fitful sleep.

Just as her son was finally losing consciousness, Ginny was waking up—a little lonely in her empty house. She went downstairs, as she did each morning, got the daily newspapers from the stoop, made coffee, and opened *The Washington Post*—as always—directly to the advice columns.

These columns were sources of comfort for Ginny; she often saw her own problems reflected in them, or at least some version of the things she was turning over in her mind. And today was an astonishing example of this. Ginny read Ann Landers with amazement. Ann's main letter was from Mary in Houston. "Dear Ann Landers," it read, "I was very upset by the debate in your column about the woman whose husband wanted her to get rid of her pets." The letter continued from there, detailing the woman's outrage, and then offering, on behalf of "animal lovers everywhere," Albert Schweitzer's "A Prayer for Animals."

Hear our humble prayer, O God, for our friends, the animals. Especially for animals who are suffering; for any that are hunted or lost or deserted or frightened or hungry; for all that must be put to death. We entreat for them all thy mercy and pity, and for those who deal with them, we ask a heart of compassion and gentle hands and kindly words. Make us, ourselves, to be true friends to animals and so to share the blessings of the merciful.

In his book *Yours Ever,* Thomas Mallon writes beautifully about letters of all kinds—including the letters written to advice columnists like Landers. "The only really difficult thing about giving advice, epistolary or otherwise," Mallon argues, "is getting people to take it." And this is precisely what Ginny did, cutting the little prayer out of the paper and writing the date in the upper-right corner. She read it aloud. Then she read it again. It was so comforting—something about the simplicity of the words, the heartfelt sentiment. Like most prayers, Schweitzer's was completely free of irony, built only from earnest entreaty—a plea for intervention.

Ginny's papers, scattered around the house in an ever-deepening, dizzying array, betrayed the variance and depth of this feeling, of the despair that Ginny was trying so assiduously to keep at arm's length. "Bless you for calling," she wrote to Dale Sweeney. "I can't stop crying—you are an angel for offering to help find Gonker. Thank you for sharing this with your brother on Calf Mountain.

I hope we can find our dear doggie." The story had so affected Dale that she'd somehow felt Gonker was her own. She'd told all her family about him, and indicated that she'd do all she could to help.

As you page through the faxes, one word springs off the page: "guidance." Ginny thanked strangers, again and again, for their guidance, guidance that they gave, in many cases, spontaneously, above and beyond what Ginny asked for. They called friends and relatives and businesses, almost as if they could see what Ginny herself was doing and wanted to mimic it. Vicki from the Rockingham/Harrisonburg SPCA called, unsolicited, and offered her advice, her experience with finding missing pets. Mary Baldwin, a career-placement officer at a local high school, also offered any assistance she could give. "I'm an animal lover," she told Ginny when she called, "and so when my husband cut the article out of the paper I couldn't help but call." In her notes, Ginny tracked each follow-up call in a new color: "Very nice lady," the document reads. "Has a beagle. Will go out looking tonight and tomorrow all day."

In several rooms, Ginny had taped the same image of Gonker on the wall. In black-and-white, but still regal-looking, he lounged on the sofa. Depending on what kind of mood Ginny was in, Gonker looked happy or sad, or—more rarely—begging for help with his eyes. *Where are you?* he seemed to say. *Why is it taking you so long?* And—as often happened in her lowest moments—Ginny heard her mother's voice, heard that drawling, almost lazy country twang: *"Well, certainly, Virginia, you'll never amount to much."* Look at how easily you're defeated. A patch of forest just a few miles long. And you let him get away. Don't you care? What kind of a mother are you? You can't even get that right.

39

Here he was, then, walking along the trail. Each paw, covered in mud, the pads of his feet—always soft— now growing more callused with each passing mile. His knees, which had once been pain-free, now ached in the morning, a deep ache within the joint itself, mysterious to him and accentuated by the cold. This boundless darkness. Every distant house—something to trot toward, but nothing more. No hope in those houses. No smell of home.

And—worse—danger. There was a scent of danger to the houses out here. Unfamiliar, these people. *I don't know anything about them.* And how to learn? With Fielding, he'd spent a lifetime learning how to coexist, to thrive. For example: Fielding always left mac and cheese in the sink. He never cleaned it up, not the first night. Not after dinner. Many nights had been spent, profitably, licking the pots clean, savoring the Kraft flavor, the salt and residual soggy pasta and milk fat. Where would the mac and cheese be out here? Even if the kitchen door was open, it wouldn't be safe to go in. There was just the darkness. The darkness and the stars in the night sky, so distant and glittering and lonely.

40

Day Nine of Search

Eleven Days Left

"Looks like rain," Fielding said, sweeping back the mildewed floral-print curtains of Room 118 at the Super 8 motel in Waynesboro.

The next day on the trail opened with a cold drizzle. The foliage, over even the course of that single week, had turned dirty brown and faded. Many of the trees were bare. A cold northern wind had swept through the valley—seemingly sent to strip the last leaves, to prepare the forest for winter.

Ranger Jennifer Waltz at the Blue Ridge National Park rangers' office had advised that Fielding stay out on the trail as much as possible. "The dog will keep on a scent and will probably stay within that scent range," the ranger had told him. "He'll key on it." And so, by day eight, Fielding's feet had blistered almost beyond recognition.

On the third day, he'd slipped in the mud and sprained his left ankle. The swelling had never gone down. John had spent afternoons resting in the hotel rooms they'd rented; Fielding had been relentless and hadn't given himself that chance.

He'd also called Noel as soon as they'd neared the area, and Noel had come out on the trail to help in the search. He'd become really enthusiastic about the entire project, and spread word to their old college friends. "Dude," he'd said to Fielding, "we'll totally have a fund-raiser, man. A big blowout, you know? Like—intense. For Gonker."

And, sure enough, Noel gathered about thirty people at his apartment on the outskirts of Charlottesville. Everyone donated at least five dollars, and by the middle of the evening there was a sizable chunk of cash. The idea was, of course, that Fielding would use the money to defray the expenses of the search. But at a certain point, the beer ran out. And Noel noticed the big, clear jar of cash sitting on the coffee table in the living room.

"To the bev center!" he yelled, holding the jar in the air. And, much to Fielding's astonishment, everyone else in the room began to cheer.

That night, Ginny drove to her favorite restaurant in McLean: Pulcinella. Pulcinella is a simple Italian place— one of the first restaurants in McLean—built in the late 1970s, a time when the town was changing from a leafy Virginia village into a full-fledged suburb of the nation's capital. Pulcinella's menu features a delicious but basic red sauce—homemade, bright and garlicky, and served over fresh pasta. And of course there's pizza from a wood-fired oven. And antipasti on a long white marble counter, many of them imported from Napoli: artichoke hearts marinated in the finest olive oil, a dozen varieties of salami, olives from the owner's family's olive orchard on the slopes of the Adriatic Sea.

Sitting in a booth by herself, Ginny ordered pasta and an iced tea. The namesake of the restaurant was the masked character from Neapolitan puppetry—Pulcinella, or Punch, the exuberant, crafty miscreant, a character sometimes depicted holding a piece of pasta and a wooden spoon. In seventeenth-century Italian commedia dell'arte, Pulcinella would often stand outside of the action and comment on it, providing a counterpoint to the improvisatory drama on the stage. On this night, Ginny reflected that Pulcinella was an appropriate avatar: she felt like she was floating above her own life, watching the story of Gonker unfold from afar.

Virginia finished her dinner and watched the restaurant empty out. She'd brought a legal pad and a pencil to jot down ideas, but now she couldn't think of anything. "What about an animal psychic?" she wrote—and then, embarrassed, erased the note. But no, no, she had to follow every lead, explore every possibility. She wrote the words down again, then sighed and looked up from the paper. On the other side of the restaurant, closest to the kitchen, the waiters had begun to put the chairs on the tables. She looked out toward the street. The windows were black lakes, reflecting some light back, letting some street light through. If last night had ended with her remembrance of her father's face, tonight was ending with the contemplation of her own. She stared at her own image. It was ghostly—partial and disembodied—and framed by the night-lit glass.

She left. And when she made it to the car, she sat behind the wheel for a long time. And then it broke—all the emotion that had been building inside of her. Sobbing in the car, alone, wiping her face with the backs of her hands, Ginny was barely able to breathe, unable to stop the tears.

"Damn dog," she said, and wiped her nose with her forearm.

41

Day Ten of Search

Ten Days Left

The pilgrimage has been around for a long time. Maybe part of its appeal comes from the way our species evolved: walking out of the Tigris-Euphrates river valley, spreading out across the world. Nearly every major religion has at least one significant pilgrimage, whether to Mecca or to Rome, and every year thousands of pilgrims make long journeys, worldwide, for the sake of faith. It's perhaps a uniquely American gesture to do a pilgrimage for the sake of nature, a pilgrimage without a religious imperative, but there you go: we love hiking—walking for long stretches of time through the forest, for the sake of nothing more than walking for long stretches of time through the forest. Or, as John Muir, the founder of the Sierra Club, wrote: "Everybody needs beauty as well as bread, places to play

in and pray in, where nature may heal and give strength
to body and soul alike."

Earl Shaffer was the first American to find that healing
and strength by walking the entirety of the Appalachian
Trail in a single season. A World War II veteran, he'd
joined the army with his best friend, Walter Winemiller.
Both Shaffer and Winemiller were posted to the Pacific
theater, but Winemiller was killed—cut down during the
first wave of the amphibious assault on Iwo Jima.

The military trained Shaffer to become a radio-and-
radar operator, and he had a brutal tour of duty, carrying heavy equipment onto beaches under the strafe of
machine-gun fire. He came out of the war confused and
depressed and—by chance—stumbled across an article
on the trail, still quite rough at that time, in a 1947 issue
of *Outdoor Life* magazine.

When Shaffer hiked the trail, the conditions were miserable. "For warmth at night," writes one biographical
sketch, "he'd pile leaves on the ground, wrap himself in
his plastic tarp and cover that with leaves, leaving only
his head sticking out. At times, he thought he was a goner.
Many times, especially in the White Mountains in New
Hampshire, he'd wrap his feet in burlap to keep them
warm."

John and Fielding didn't wrap their feet (or Uli's) in
burlap. But the walking—combined with the deteriora-
tion of Fielding's health—did take its toll on them. There
is only so much that you can do, even if you have deep
optimism and devotion to a cause. Eventually, you have

to surrender. You have to weigh costs and benefits, and make difficult decisions. Fielding did have to go back to work. And so: John and Fielding returned. They'd burned through hundreds of dollars, and hundreds of hours. They'd searched up and down the strip of trail near the place where Gonker had disappeared. They had not been triumphant—not even close. And, unlike a different kind of pilgrimage, there'd been no moment of transcendence at the center of their experience. They hadn't kissed a holy black stone, or a sacred icon, or a shrouded relic.

At the door to the house, Ginny greeted them both. She gave them a hug—first her son, then John. They didn't say anything. They went inside. As they crossed the threshold, the clocks began to chime the hour. Seven in the evening. A cascading, rolling sequence of sounds, beginning with the cuckoos and working gradually toward the 1820 Lancaster County mahogany longcase. They'd almost run out of days. Gonker's calendar was approaching zero.

42

THURSDAY, OCTOBER 22, 1998

Day Eleven of Search

Nine Days Left

As the hours passed, as the 21st turned into the 22nd and the day slipped into night, a sense of doom and loss settled over the Marshall household. The symptoms of Gonker's Addison's disease would by now probably have begun to manifest. Soon, he'd feel the fatigue of his body's impending collapse. He would be puzzled, perhaps, by his sudden weakening. It would seem like a weight on the body, a physical diminishment through force, the ground wanting to claim him for its own. Fielding imagined Gonker, struggling to walk. Gonker, unable to lift himself with the morning light, wanting only to lie in a sunny space on a hillside and close his eyes—and rest.

Do animals have consciousness of self? The animals you love—the dogs and cats and mice and rabbits and canaries—do they understand themselves the way you do? These are, of course, impossibly broad questions—ones that are debated constantly by philosophers and psychologists and evolutionary biologists and cognitive neuroscientists and artists and primatologists. Is consciousness the "leading edge of perceptual memory," as the philosopher Michael Lockwood suggests? Is consciousness the snap of a photographer's lens? Is it, as William James said, an exception from the "original chaos" of life, the moment where something "entirely new" "seems to slip in"? For Gonker, on the Appalachian Trail, did his loneliness—the first time he'd been alone like that, really alone—mean he discovered some new part of himself, some beautiful doggish pocket of self? One that wasn't so in love with doughnuts?

He walked and walked. He must have—in some way—thought about the things that were there and the things that weren't; he certainly investigated the scents of the world. His olfactory membrane—as big as an unfurled handkerchief—struggled to categorize and understand the things he encountered. He was a dog and he was walking. He was walking and looking for Fielding and Ginny and John and Uli and home.

Driving to work that first day back, Fielding negotiated the heavy traffic on Leesburg Pike, inching past the half-dozen car dealerships and the newly built Booz Allen office building. Gridlock. He turned the radio on. He turned the radio off. He turned it on again. The heat from the heater was *too* hot, the open window too cold, too drafty. His skin was uncomfortable; he could feel it draped on his bones. He was about to merge onto the beltway and get in the stream of traffic headed downtown when he had a sudden idea.

He turned the steering wheel and, crossing the median, performed an illegal U-turn on Chain Bridge Road. He sped in the opposite direction—away from traffic—and scanned the buildings for one that he remembered from long ago, from the day in 1985 when the family had adopted Benson. After two miles or so, there it was. He pulled into the driveway of the Humane Society of Fairfax County.

Fielding went up to the front desk, looking no doubt a little wild-eyed. "I'd like to volunteer to walk a dog," he said. It felt a little bit like a bank robbery, but the receptionist just smiled and handed him a nicely printed volunteer application.

"We'll have to get you booked for an orientation," she said—and then he was nodding, and setting up the appointment for a week later, for Thursday, October 29. He filled out the paperwork.

You hear the stories all the time: the person who never wanted kids—*never*—but then, at forty, adopted a dog, and went mad for it, loved it with all the depth and power available to a human being. It is the need to nurture, to give compassionately to another creature. "Empathy," writes Sue Monk Kidd, "is the most mysterious transaction the human soul can have."

Ginny began her last round of faxes. "If he has died," she wrote to the Greene County dog warden, "we would like his remains so that we could give him a proper burial."

But she kept on working. There were a lot of things in the world that Ginny couldn't change. Her life had been full of unfairness, full of terrible memories. If there was a chance she could save a dog, then she would try her hardest to save a dog. As long as there was still any chance, she would treat Gonker the way she wished she'd been treated as a child. She would make up for the smallest sliver of all of the injustice in the world. And so somehow this act became a defense not just of a single creature but of helpless creatures everywhere.

That night, back at his apartment, Fielding called Peyton.

"Gonker?" she said, answering on the second ring. "Is that you?"

"Woof," Fielding said.

"Did you find him?"

"Woof."

"And you're sure there's been no ransom note?"

"Woof."

"If you're totally losing your mind, bark once."

"Woof."

"I always thought you were part animal, Fields. You know that, right?"

Fielding laughed quietly, more of a murmur. "Undomesticated," he said, and sighed. "Right to the end."

43

Day Twelve of Search
_____
Eight Days Left

In a final effort, Ginny put together a full-page ad in the *News Leader*. She prepared the text, dwelling on the heartbreaking specifics of his appearance: "His ears are floppy and he has a long tail. His fur is soft and silky to the touch," she wrote. In that word, "floppy," you can hear the sadness, the intimacy of her voice, the stewardship that she feels for this creature. It is certainly a mother's love. "If he is dead," Ginny's ad concludes, "then please help us find his body. It's the not knowing where he is—or if he is alive—that tears at our hearts."

And yet she couldn't completely give up hope. Not publicly, at least. "We are running out of time—and options," Ginny faxed to the *News Leader*, inquiring after the possibility that any responses, any tips, had come into the newsroom. To the Wildlife Center of Virginia, a hospital for native wildlife located in Waynesboro, Ginny wrote, "We are running out of time to find him safe & sound & are desperate to bring him home."

The not knowing—this was the most difficult part to endure. She wandered around the house. She walked down the stairs, past the dark wood of the curved stair-case railing. She walked from the formal dining room into the orange-tiled kitchen. There was the long sweep of windows in front of which she normally stood, watching the sunlight and the bluebirds, the scrub forest that sloped away behind the house. Today, it brought her no solace.

"Maybe he's in a different part of the trail entirely," Fielding said when he came over that night. He walked into the kitchen and stared at the map of the state of Vir-ginia. Fielding looked around the room at the mounds of paperwork—the sent faxes, the letters, the notes. "Maybe if we looked over the border, to the north?"

"Fields," Ginny said. She started to say something but then—stopped. "Let's talk about something else," she said.

Fielding wouldn't let it go, however. He kept circling back to images from that morning on the trail. He felt trapped in that single moment. It seemed almost like, if he could just find the right way to think about it, then the outcome would change. The memory would be altered. The dog wouldn't be lost. Gonker would bound out of the forest, happy and hungry and covered in mud. Light-headed from his own lack of food—he hadn't eaten anything in two days—Fielding barely had the energy to sit at the table.

Beside him, Ginny thought suddenly of a day in May—during that first year when Fielding had lived at home. She'd taken Gonker to the Great Falls Animal Hospital for a checkup. When she had checked in and sat down in a chair in the waiting room, she'd expected Gonker to situate himself at her feet. Instead, he'd leapt up onto his own chair—right next to Ginny. He'd crossed his front paws, one over the other, and had sat there waiting, just another patient in a doctor's office, his head held high. This became their ritual at Great Falls; when Gonker arrived, he went immediately to the receptionist, collected a dog biscuit, and then selected a chair in which to sit. Ginny liked to imagine him thinking: *I don't know what all these dogs are doing here, but I'm certainly not one of them.*

Ginny exhaled. She stood up and, suddenly resolute, walked to her corkboard. She edited her top notecard somewhat, adding two more underlines and an exclamation point.

<u>TEAM OF HEROES</u>!

Rosa Lee Chittum
Bill Kirby and The News Virginian
Mary Kay
Jenni @ The Inn at Afton
Connie Baber
Laurie at Rodes Farm Stables

She stepped back and looked at the door. Then she took out two more notecards. She wrote "John Marshall" on one. She liked the look of it like that, with his first and last names. And then, on the second, she wrote just one word: "Fielding."

44

Day Thirteen of Search

Seven Days Left

Throughout the ordeal of losing Gonker, John had stood—resolute, cheerful—at the center of the family. His confidence that the dog would be found (he exclaimed, at many points, exactly this, in a booming voice: "The dog will be found!") suffused Ginny, gave her strength during her efforts.

Determination, optimism, resolve. Much has been written, in the late twentieth and early twenty-first centuries, about the effects of optimism on a life. Countless studies have linked a positive mind-set to quicker recovery from illness. Since its publication in 1952, Dr. Norman Vincent Peale's *The Power of Positive Thinking* has sold over five million copies. Not to mention the multi-billion-dollar self-help industry, which is built primarily around extolling the benefits of hopeful thinking. In recent years, dozens of titles, such as *Rainy Brain, Sunny Brain: How to Retrain Your Brain to Overcome Pessimism and Achieve a More Positive Outlook,* have flooded the literary marketplace. "The brain is organized," writes Tali Sharot in her book *The Optimism Bias,* "in a way that enables optimistic beliefs to change the way we view and interact with the world around us, making optimism a self-fulfilling prophecy."

Of course, there has been a backlash. In his 2010 book, *The Uses of Pessimism and the Danger of False Hope,* the conservative English thinker Roger Scruton tries to "show the place of pessimism in restoring balance and wisdom to the conduct of human affairs." He traces what he believes to be an optimism epidemic throughout world history, and outlines a way of thinking in a darker and more disciplined way. Only through balanced thinking, Scruton argues, can we achieve good results.

John Marshall, however, did not agree with this idea.

Fielding, too, appreciated John's steadfast positivity. He was the best search companion that Fielding could have wished for; the mystery of the disappearance became something for them to unravel together—father and son traveling through rural Virginia. And then, when it was time to go back home, John did so, unwilling to push beyond the limits of common sense.

"Remember, Fielding," he said, on the night of October 24, sitting on the couch in the basement rec room. The Marshalls had recorded that Thursday's episode of *ER* to watch together, as a family, but the show remained paused on the big-screen television, the credits frozen in place. John was full of enthusiasm. He was waving the remote control like some kind of conductor's baton. "Remember," he repeated, "the ancient Druids persevered in the face of many different kinds of obstacles."

"The Druids?" Fielding said.

"Absolutely," John said. "They're our ancestors. And—they were the first to keep animals as pets. That's a known fact."

"Dad," Fielding said, "you're making that up."

"The Druids were a solemn people, Fielding," John said. "We stand in their great footprints. I would never joke about the Druids."

"Is that supposed to make me feel better?"

John frowned. "Well, I think so," he said. "It's not working?"

"It's not working," Fielding said.

"Then let's go outside."

And before either Ginny or Fielding could object, John had dashed up the stairs and opened the front door. They followed. All three of them stood in the semicircle of the driveway. It was raining; the rain was thick, falling in a saturating dense mist. They all shivered.

"John," Ginny said, "get an umbrella."

"No time! No time!" John said. "We have to call to Gonker through the mysterious darkness."

"I think Dad's lost it," Fielding said.

"Should we carry him back inside?" Ginny asked.

But John wouldn't be dissuaded. "Gonker!" he yelled.

"Gonker!" The remote was still in his hand. He turned and pointed it at his son. "Come on!" he yelled. "Gonker! Where are you? Gonker!"

Across the street, the light went on in the Elmores' living room.

"Someone's going to call the cops," Ginny said.

But this was McLean, after all. Nothing but winding, digressing roads, and large estates on wooded parcels of land. The nearest police station was twenty minutes from the Marshalls' leafy cul-de-sac. And so, reluctantly at first, but then with increasing enthusiasm, Fielding and Ginny joined in: "Gonker!" they yelled. "Gonker!"

There they were, standing in the October evening, hundreds of miles from where that dog might be. There was no chance he could hear them. It was a ridiculous thing to do. But soon they were crying, laughing, coughing—their faces wet with rain. "Gonker!" they bellowed. "Gonker! Where are you?"

PART 5

Endings

What will end
our sadness?

The hours
passing

Blow out the sun!
Blow out the moon!
Only the dog
is a pure work of God!

—JESSE NATHAN

45

The answer, it turns out, was this: he was eating garbage at a ski resort.

At two in the morning on October 25—only hours after the Marshalls had yelled into the rainy darkness—the phone rang one last time. Ginny almost didn't answer it. She let it ring and ring. John stirred only slightly, rolling away from the noise. Finally, Ginny reached over. "Marshall residence," she said, sighing, her voice tired and gravelly with sleep.

"Mrs. Marshall," an alert and happy-sounding voice said on the other end of the line, "this is Sergeant Wade with the Wintergreen Police Department."

Ginny sat up.

"Go ahead," she said.

"Mrs. Marshall," Sergeant Wade said, "we believe we've located your missing golden retriever, Bonker?"

"Gonker."

"I'm sorry, ma'am?"

"His name is Gonker," Ginny said, "and I'm afraid to ask if he's alive."

The officer laughed. "He's very much alive, ma'am, but we're unable to bring him in. He's holed up in the woods behind one of our properties here at Wintergreen."

Wintergreen Resort is a large recreational community near Charlottesville. It has four mountains with ski trails, three golf courses, and a full-service spa. It has hundreds of condos, mixed in with large private estates, and—more important for a lost dog—many thousands of trash cans, an ample nighttime buffet.

"One of our officers—Spanky Harris—tried to call to him, but he ran away."

"Now," Ginny said, remembering all the false leads, "you're certain it's him."

"Fairly certain, ma'am."

And so Sergeant Wade went on to describe the situation. Earlier that week, some residents of Wintergreen had read about Gonker in the paper. The next day, they'd seen a dog matching his description and called the resort police. The resort police had arrived on scene, but they'd also been unable to get Gonker into the squad car. One thing they'd noticed without doubt, however, was his purple-and-white herringbone collar.

Gonker was alive!

Despite the hour—despite her exhaustion and fear and doubt—Ginny was filled with an unruly wash of exhilaration. John was awake, huddled against her, listening intently to the conversation. When she hung up the phone, he let out a whoop of joy. He stood up on the mattress—and began to do a kind of wild, embarrassing dance.

"The camel!" he yelled. "The caravansary! Caesar's generals!"

"Hush," Ginny said. "It's not a sure thing."

"We've got him," John said, "the elusive little bastard."

But Ginny ignored this. She slipped out of bed. There was something she needed to see—one thing, immediately—just before she called Fielding. She walked through the darkened hallways of the house and descended the main stairs.

In the kitchen, she reached for and found the little light on the round, map-covered table. She sat in the straight-backed wooden chair, took out her reading glasses, and squinted down at the key of the Rand McNally. She used a pencil and the edge of a piece of paper to make a hasty measurement.

He'd gone 111 miles.

Gonker went missing on October 10 near Catawba, Virginia. He'd been found, fourteen days later, at Wintergreen Resort. The distance between the two locations was roughly 111 miles. And that was assuming a straight line, which was, obviously, an impossibility. This meant that the dog had covered at least seven miles a day, searching—Ginny imagined—for home. He'd followed, roughly, the path of the Appalachian Trail, heading north-northwest. Ginny was certain that Gonker had gone looking for Fielding, that he'd been searching for them these past two weeks as hard as they'd been searching for him.

John came downstairs. He stood in the doorway to the

kitchen. Unable to contain himself, he'd been the one to place the call to their son.

"He's already on the road," John said. "He'll be there before sunrise."

Ginny nodded. "John," she said. "Look at this." She pointed to the map, where she'd marked out Gonker's path.

"A hundred and eleven miles," she said to her husband. "I just can't believe it."

"Well, Ginny," John said, taking her in his arms, "neither can Gonker."

46

Fielding rushed to Wintergreen, hoping that this lost-dog story—unlike so many others—would indeed have a happy ending. He called the resort police and established Gonker's location: White Oak Drive, in a neighborhood on the perimeter of the resort property.

Fielding listened to the radio as he drove up there, the stars a broad canvas above the roof of the car. Slowly, the smallest margin of sunlight crept into the sky; the world began to awake. He found the address of the couple, Trent and Laurie Bowen, who'd reported Gonker to the resort police. Finally, at the house in question, Fielding stopped the car, climbed out, and stretched—tired after his four-hour drive. He had called the Bowens from a pay phone, and so they came out to greet him as he pulled up.

The three of them stood there, peering into the darkness of the woods behind the house.

And then: there he was.

Healthy-seeming and bright-eyed and twenty feet away, Gonker poked his head out of the undergrowth at the perimeter of the forest.

He looked at Fielding—and seemed to register nothing.

"Gonker!" Fielding yelled, his own voice from the previous evening echoing through his head. "Gonker!"

And at that moment—the second time Fielding called his name—Gonker leapt upward with joy. He let out a staccato yelp, tossing his head to one side, his eyes as wide as they possibly could go. He had Fielding's scent now, for sure, and he bolted toward his owner, running faster than Fielding had ever seen him run. Dog and owner collided next to the car, in the little subdivision cul-de-sac, and fell to the ground in a heap.

Gonker, Fielding immediately realized, had somehow not lost weight during his long ordeal. In fact, the next day, when Gonker went to the vet for his shot, he would weigh in one pound heavier than at his last appointment. He also smelled terrible—but Fielding didn't care. He grabbed handfuls of Gonker's fur and held him tight.

Gonker was coming home.

47

The most remarkable moment of the story, however, happened in front of a suburban home in McLean, Virginia. This moment was a rift, a cut in the fabric of time, in the consistent progress of life from one event to the next. It was a moment when a mother—a fifty-seven-year-old woman—was transformed, instantaneously, into a young girl, on a lawn, cradling a lost dog in her arms. Falling to the grass. Holding him close. He was back. Impossibly back. After all these years—through all these lives—he had returned to her. His spirit, the essence of his consciousness, had floated, untethered in the universe, for half a century. And now: fistfuls of dog fur, paws on her chest, the scent of the dirt, the scent of fertilizer, and open space, and the Appalachian woods. Oji licking her face, nipping at her chin, nuzzling her.

Fielding stood there and watched Virginia's transformation. He was arrested by it—transfixed. The weak feeling in his legs momentarily vanished. In his enthusiasm, Gonker knocked Ginny over, and her hair—which had been up in a bun—came unknotted. He nuzzled her face.

He licked her ears, her nose, her eyes. She held on to his legs, taking one in each hand. She looked up at her son.

"His paws," she said.

"I know," Fielding said.

They were rough, and the pads had been lacerated on the trail. When she tried to look more closely at one of them, though, Gonker whimpered and pulled it away. Ginny was astonished at how good he looked, though, after being out in the wilderness for over two weeks. He ambled over to the bushes and, rummaging around in there, found a long stick. He carried it over to her and dropped it on her lap. He stepped back. *Fetch?* he suggested with a short bark. And then another bark. *Fetch?*

48

The way home, then—for Ginny and Fielding and Gonker—came through the efforts of everyday people. Writers at newspapers, employees at animal hospitals, residents of a ski resort—they all helped bring the dog back.

The Daily Progress did a follow-up piece on October 28, updating its readers about the search. If Ginny and John thought that the phone calls had been heavy in the days after the first piece, this was a deluge; nearly everyone whom Ginny had contacted called to congratulate her on finding Gonker. But beyond the people to whom Ginny had talked in her fourteen days of relentless hunting, other people, total strangers, were calling to talk with her. These were secondary or tertiary contacts—people *someone else* had given Ginny's number to, and who'd helped out in the search.

"It's like an army was out there," John said to Ginny after one of these phone calls, "and we didn't even know it. The team delivered!"

"And they deserve all the credit," Ginny said.

"Take credit when the sun shines," John said, wiping tears from the corners of his eyes, "because they'll blame you when it rains."

The work of everyday people, in Ginny's mind, could not go unnoted. This was, after all, turning into a story about the kindness of strangers, about people hoping to help someone—and some animal—that they didn't know. And so Ginny began an equally massive campaign of thank-you-note writing. Everyone—all her heroes—Rosa Lee Chittum, Mary Kay, Jenni at the Inn at Afton, Ranger Waltz. Even Ann Landers. Ginny wrote notes to everyone with whom she'd spoken—everyone who'd inspired her—spending hundreds of dollars on cards and stamps. "Fantastic," she scrawled in her notes from her second conversation with the Blue Ridge Ranger Station. "Ecstatic," she wrote on the page recording her talk with the Shenandoah Park ranger. "So happy. I wish every dog story had a happy ending," scrawled Laurie at Rodes Farm Stables at the top of one of her pages and pages of notes.

On November 24, *The Daily Progress* ran this letter:

Wandering pooch was lucky to get lost in Charlottesville area

To the many residents of the Charlottesville area who helped my son, Fielding Marshall, find his dog Gonker recently after being lost 15 days on the Appalachian Trail, the entire Marshall family wants to say a great big thank you.

Our special thanks goes to Bryan McKenzie of *The Daily Progress* for his very kind column on Oct. 21. "Wandering pooch has pal worried." He alerted the Charlottesville community about my son's plight and the fact that his dog needed medication—and soon— to survive.

Mr. McKenzie's follow-up story on Oct. 28 ("Man catches up with his best friend") was another sensitive account telling everyone that Gonker had been found and how both dog and owner were doing.

During the long two-week period that Gonker was missing, my son and I talked to many residents in and around Charlottesville. In addition, my son spent many days posting missing-dog flyers together with my husband, and searching throughout your community. Each of you was so helpful and encouraging.

Many residents in the Charlottesville area also called us with possible leads and advice. It felt so comforting to know they were all on the lookout to help us find Gonker. We were running out of hope and Gonker was running out of time. It was not knowing where Gonker was that tore at our hearts.

The Wintergreen Police gave us the big break we needed to locate Gonker. Officer Spanky Harris determined it was my son's dog he had been seeing around and called us. Then Sgt. Gary Wade called us early one morning to say he thought Gonker was on a particular street. I know both gentlemen spent a lot of time trying to coax the dog to come to them.

The entire Wintergreen Police Department took our concern seriously and did a lot of asking around and looking for us.

These gentlemen deserve a lot of credit—they are the real heroes to the Marshall family and we wanted you to take pride in knowing what they had done for us.

Our prayers are answered. Our heartfelt thanks to all of you as well. It is indeed a miracle that my son was able to find his dog. I hope the next dog to get lost has the good fortune to get lost in the Charlottesville area because I know the community will help show him the way back home.

—Virginia C. Marshall
Fairfax County

49

That Thanksgiving, Fielding—having in fact retained his job—had the holiday off. He decided to spend the night in McLean, so that Gonker and Uli could play together in the evening *and* the morning. They liked to sleep in a pile at the foot of his bed, after running until they couldn't run any longer.

In the darkness just before midnight on Wednesday—the air filled with the sound of two snoring dogs—Fielding called Peyton. They'd been trying to get in touch with one another since October but just missing each other, playing a cross-continental game of phone tag.

"Hey, Monkey Boy," Peyton said when she answered. "I heard you found your dog."

"We lured him out of the woods," Fielding said, "with a pound of French fries and a case of Michelob."

"I heard that. Mom said he's got a beer gut now."

"We should have used Michelob Light," Fielding said.

"You're famous, too. She said you were on the local news?"

"It was mostly Dad."

"Oh no."

"Yep," Fielding said. "It was just like you're imagining. He sang a song called 'Hope Is Never Lost.' "

"No."

"Yes. He said the ancient Etruscans used to howl like dogs to give thanks to the god of the sun."

"Is that true?"

"Not as far as I can tell," Fielding said.

Peyton described what she'd been doing for the past year. She'd just written her first novel—a book based on a true story about an exploding whale carcass on an Oregon beach. "I think it's an abysmal failure," she concluded cheerfully.

"Keep trying," Fielding said.

"That's exactly what Dad told me," Peyton said.

They talked about how strange it was for Fielding to be back together with Gonker, and how normal everything seemed. The dog's health had actually deteriorated a bit, Fielding admitted. He seemed a bit stiffer and slower; once, when Fielding had picked him up, Gonker had inexplicably yelped with pain. He'd just been to the vet, where they'd increased his dosage of the synthetic hormone. From the annual blood panel that they did, they felt that his condition was quite possibly worsening. This news had made Fielding somber, and had cast something of a pall over his holiday. Though he was trying his best to care for Gonker, he wondered if the hours alone, when Fielding was at work, were having a gradual, cumulative effect on the dog.

"And how are *you* feeling?" Peyton asked.

"I've been better." He paused. "But—I think I've developed a plan."

After the Thanksgiving meal, the Marshalls gathered again in that main room—Ginny with her white wine and black-currant syrup, Fielding and John with cups of mulled cider. They recounted the events of the last few months. John was astounded to hear of Gonker's extreme thirst upon being rescued; when Fielding finally got the golden retriever in the car, Gonker drank a gallon jug of water, without stopping.

Ginny told the story—which she'd forgotten in the tumult of the search—of how their neighbors had enlisted the help of the local Mormon elders, who'd started a Mormon prayer chain, on the family's behalf. Was *this* the thing that had tipped the balance in their favor? Who could really be sure, after all?

Gonker sat beside them, warmed by the fire. He seemed to be listening. At some point, he rested his head on his crossed front paws. Uli lay next to him, in turn. He was soon unconscious—sprawled near his friend, his back touching Gonker's side. Since Gonker's return, neither dog liked to be alone in a room; they'd seek each other out, whenever possible; they'd even started sharing the same oversized dog bed.

Fielding finished his cider. He cleared his throat.

"Mom," he said, a gulf opening somewhere inside of

him and expanding through his chest. "I'm not feeling well." And so it all came out—the torrent of symptoms, the months and months of suffering.

Ginny was quiet. Her body was still but her mind was frantic. She was reevaluating a dozen moments with her son—looks of pain, or fatigue, or even unreadable looks, moments when she hadn't been able tell what was going on with him. John shook his head.

"Oh, Fielding," he said, "that's just awful."

"Which part?"

"All of it."

"Well," Ginny said, "how can we help?" She was wide-eyed. "We know a specialist, actually. A gastroenterologist. He lives just down the street—next to the Olshans."

"That's okay, Mom."

"I could call him," Ginny said.

"No, Mom. I can handle it."

"I can give you his number. It would take a few minutes to call. You can describe your symptoms to him, and—"

"Mom—"

"—you don't have to commit to an appointment, right away."

"Mom—"

"It would just be a small thing—"

"Look, Mom, I was wondering: Could Gonker stay here for a while? Until I get well."

A log hissed on the hearth. The dry oak cracked—and a bright-red ember fell away from the burning wood. Ginny looked at her son.

"Oh, Fielding," she said, after a moment, her eyes filling with tears, "we would be honored."

In her book, *Inside of a Dog,* Alexandra Horowitz writes about the behavior of dogs, marveling at how complex—and often underestimated—the animals are. She points out that the word "domesticated" "grew from a root form meaning 'belonging to the house.'" Gonker, then, belonged to the Marshalls' house, in the deepest sense of that word. It's striking, after all, that the Latinate names for the dog, for all of the dogs that live in our midst, contain such a strong piece of messaging: *Canis lupus familiaris.*

What had Gonker seen out there, out in the woods? Had he chased coyotes, or been chased by them, or merely heard their mournful howls in the darkness of the woods at night? Maybe the very fact that he couldn't tell his story, that he simply couldn't gain access to the language for it, was part of what made people react with such generosity, time and time again. Maybe they—like Rosa Lee Chittum—sensed his powerlessness before the cruelties of fate. And saw their own powerlessness, reflected back to them.

Familiar. Horowitz asks, "What do dogs know . . . about themselves, about right and wrong, about emergencies, emotions, and death?" The great mystery, of course, the one that will never be solved, is exactly what happened to Gonker out there on the Appalachian Trail.

When he returned to the Marshall family, he could only resume his place in their daily lives. He had no language to explain what he'd been through, and the Marshalls had no language to explain to him how hard they'd tried to bring him home.

50

On an unusually warm day that December, the phone rang at the Marshall residence. Ginny answered.

"Mrs. Marshall?" the voice on the other end of the line said. It was a gruff voice, a man's voice, not unlike many of the voices that had phoned in false leads throughout those weeks in October.

"Speaking."

"Well, Mrs. Marshall," the man said, "I found your phone number again when I was cleaning out my wallet, and I decided that I had to call."

"Yes?" Ginny said. "What would you like to tell me?"

"Well, ma'am. I hope I'm not troubling you. It's about your son's dog, Gonker." The man paused. "I can't get him out of my mind. I read that article in the paper a few months back, and the whole time now, I've been wondering: Was he ever found?"

Ginny smiled. She didn't miss a beat.

"Why, yes," she said. "Yes, he was."

"No foolin'?" the man said, his voice rising at least an octave.

"No foolin', indeed," Ginny said. She smiled.

"Well, ma'am," he said, "that news just made my Christmas."

51

Even good dogs get old.

The average life span of a golden retriever is eleven years; Gonker lived exactly that long. By 2003, his eyesight had failed. His liver and kidneys, weakened by years of medication for his Addison's, started to malfunction. His hips throbbed with arthritis; he struggled to walk, or even stand. Uli would nudge his friend in the ribs gently, trying to get him to play, but he would refuse. By May, Gonker could barely get out the door. By June, he had to be carried over the threshold and placed on the grass in the sun, just so he could keep warm. By the beginning of July, Ginny knew it was time to say goodbye.

Fielding came over in the morning. He sat with his old friend on the stoop of the doorway. He had Gonker's head in his lap, and he was petting the dog's soft gray-and-yellow ears.

"I talked with Noel this morning," he whispered.

Gonker raised an eyebrow.

"He told me to say"—and here Fielding started to lose his composure—" 'Safe travels, man.' " He blew his nose on the sleeve of his shirt. "You know how he talks. 'Tell him: Safe travels, man, wherever you might go.'"

Gonker relaxed the eyebrow.

"It seems like a good message, right, buddy?"

John walked over and stood behind Fielding. He put his hands on his son's shoulders. "I love you, Fielding," he said. And then father and son picked Gonker up and carried him out to the car. Ginny walked beside them. They situated him in Ginny's lap, in the passenger seat, and they rolled down the window. And then—very slowly—they drove through the neighborhood, showing Gonker all of the sights he'd grown accustomed to seeing, all of the places that he'd loved, that—for years—he'd trotted happily by. Now he only just managed to wag his tail.

John drove. Ginny cradled Gonker close to her body. Fielding sat behind them, his seat belt off, leaning forward into the space between the two front seats. Ginny wanted to keep everyone there, exactly like that, to hold on to that instant, forever. Of course, it was impossible. As she herself often said when confronted by impermanence, quoting the hymn: "Time, like an ever-rolling stream, bears all its sons away." She petted Gonker's head, stroking the velvety softness of his ears. She scratched underneath his chin.

The veterinarian—Dr. Henshaw, Gonker's longtime clinician at Great Falls Animal Hospital—came over to the house. The Marshalls sat down with their beloved dog, his body sprawled across Fielding's and Ginny's legs. Working briskly, the veterinarian administered the

Euthasol into Gonker's front paw. The medicine worked within seconds. Gonker's body twitched once, and then his head fell onto Ginny's lap. He was gone.

In death, the body of someone you love is always a shock. It is so familiar. You expect it to stand, to open its eyes, to talk, to fill with the life, the spirit, that you know so well. But it doesn't. It remains immobile, inert. It is heavy in a way that's almost impossible to understand.

The veterinarian waited a few minutes, in silence. Then he packed up his things and got ready to go. He asked Ginny what she was planning to do with the body. When she told him, he said that it was his duty to inform her that a McLean town ordinance prohibited the burial of pets on private land. Ginny nodded, thanked him for that piece of information, and walked with him to his car.

And so—Gonker's final resting place? It's a secret.

52

Later that year, Ginny opened the mailbox and found a letter—addressed to the whole family—from the Virginia-Maryland Regional College of Veterinary Medicine at Virginia Tech University. Dean Peter Eyre was writing to inform her that the Great Falls Animal Hospital had made a donation in Gonker's name to the university's Veterinary Memorial Fund.

Ginny was astonished. She sat down, fittingly, at the kitchen table, and wrote a letter of thanks.

September 2003
Dear Friends at Great Falls Animal Hospital,

Imagine our surprise yesterday when we received a letter from the Dean at Virginia Tech's Veterinary College. He said that a donation to the Veterinary Memorial Fund had been made in Gonker's name by the Doctors and Staff at Great Falls.

You could have knocked us over with a feather! Such a thoughtful and meaningful way for you to remember one very special "fur person." The Marshall family—Fields, Ginny, John, and Peyton—thank you for your kindness.

Maybe Virginia Tech will discover a cure for Addison's Disease one day. Wouldn't that be a wonderful accomplishment? Gonker would wag his tail to hear that news!

I miss my friends at Great Falls Animal Hospital. I hope everything is going well for all of you. You always fussed over Gonker (and me). As a result, I think he actually looked forward—somewhat—to getting his monthly shot. And wasn't Gonker a character? Didn't you love the way he sat in the chair, waiting for his name to be called?

As you can probably imagine, things are kinda quiet around here without our beloved doggie. Even now, two months after we had to say goodbye, we catch ourselves looking for him when we come in the door.

Once again, a special thank you to Dr. Henshaw.

I think we all worked together to help Gonker have a wonderful life.

With affection for you all,
The Entire Marshall Family

53

It was September 5, 2003. Al Qaeda leader Osama bin Laden declared that his priority was, in the near future, to use biological weapons on the United States. Hurricane Fabian hit Bermuda—a Category 3 storm, with winds in excess of 120 miles per hour—the strongest hurricane to strike that island nation in fifty years. North Korea's Supreme People's Assembly re-elected Kim Jong-Il as chairman of the National Defense Commission in, surprisingly, a unanimous vote. A case of SARS—sudden acute respiratory syndrome, responsible for over eight thousand deaths in Canada, China, Hong Kong, the Philippines, Taiwan, the United States, and Vietnam—was first discovered in Singapore.

Dutch pharmacies had just become the first in the world to sell marijuana as a pharmaceutical drug. Zimbabwe's only opposition newspaper closed. Arnold Schwarzenegger kicked off his campaign to run for the governorship of the State of California in the recall election. A Viking warrior's remains were discovered in Dublin. Mars passed the Earth at a distance of roughly fifty-five million kilometers—the closest it had been in nearly sixty thousand years.

And—in the interstellar vastness—a single dog's soul—a humble, meager creature—slipped away from its body, disintegrating and rising outward, becoming its natural self. First, it spent a few weeks tumbling—rising and rolling and falling—along the dirt-hewn pathways of the Appalachian Trail. It was a puff—a corona—of sub-atomic dust. It lingered there for a while. But then it had other business to attend to. It took off. And that's when it began to really travel.

Epilogue

Roger, of course, thought that I was simply wasting my mornings. However, he did not desert me, but lay under the table asleep while I wrestled with my work.

—GERALD DURRELL, *My Family and Other Animals*

Laska ran joyfully and anxiously through the slush that swayed beneath her.

—LEO TOLSTOY, *Anna Karenina*

Levin's dog, Laska, running through the marsh, has always been one of my favorite passages in *Anna Karenina*. It shows Tolstoy at his best. It's the opposite, in many ways, of the hundred-page epilogue to *War and Peace*, where he bludgeons his readers with a treatise on human power and the nature of historical change.

Rendering Laska, Tolstoy is subtle, sweet, imaginative. The semi-articulate patterns of human consciousness are hard enough to capture on the page; encapsulating the ways a dog thinks—as a human artist—is an even bigger challenge. But there she is. Laska—alive, eager, quavering, joyful, encountering the world primarily through her sense of smell.

I've lived with—and lost—beloved dogs, several of them, over the years. I'm still haunted by the dog to whom I never got to say goodbye: Glasgow, my St. Bernard. I had to give her up for adoption when I was unable to care for her, in March of 2005. Though I was able to find a good home for Glasgow—a farm in Vermont where she lived out a happy, roaming, muddy existence—my last image of her, the image of a dog looking back at me with confused eyes as her new family drove her away, will never dissipate. It still constricts my chest when I imagine it, today: Glasgow in the back of the truck, closing her muzzle and sniffing for my disappearing scent, shifting her weight and looking for me as she drove away.

Embedded reporters are rarely *actually* embedded with their subjects; I awake every morning next to Peyton Marshall, my wife—and the mother of our six-year-old twins.

Over the years, taking our children to their grandparents' house in McLean, I couldn't help noticing, on nearly every flat surface, the photographs of the large, cheerful-looking dog, stick in mouth, tongue hanging lazily to one side. I mentioned these photos to Peyton. She rolled her eyes. "There are more pictures of Gonker," she said, "than there are of me or Fielding or Dad."

And so I counted. And—by a small margin—she was right.

Stories tighten the fabric of a family. Ginny, John, and subsequently Fielding were eager to tell me the Gonker story. But its background—Ginny's childhood, Fielding's attempt at parenting, his crushing illness—came more slowly, over many years.

Fielding, it turned out, had ulcerative colitis. He was sick, persistently and deeply ill, until 2003, when he went to the Cleveland Clinic—immediately after Gonker's death—and had surgery to remove the bulk of his large intestine. At his thinnest, he weighed less than 145 pounds. He nearly died. It entailed a deep kind of trust, telling me these difficult stories. I hope that I have proved worthy of them.

Even now, many years later, the megaphone that John used on the trail is displayed prominently at the Marshall residence. It reminds the family—whenever they see it— of their shared past. This is the way that objects live in our midst. They accumulate life unexpectedly. It adheres to them. That megaphone became a living thing, a referent to a lost time, to the idea of a father and son, together, searching for something in a treacherous landscape.

Thanks

I'd like to thank, first of all, my hero/agent Bill Clegg, who sold this book while I was crossing Morocco in a bus without any cell-phone reception. Equally deep thanks to my hero/editor Tim O'Connell, whose formal, and informal, notes helped shape and transform the project. Robin Desser provided invaluable comments as well, and my thanks go out to her. To my mentor and former editor Shaye Areheart, thank you for believing in me and continuing to give me the kind of support that a writer so badly needs. And, of course, many thanks to the artist Margaret Owen, whose illustrations added so much to the manuscript.

I completed part of this book at the Hawthornden International Retreat for Writers. To Mrs. Drue Heinz, whose generosity in service of literature is deep and abiding, my heartfelt appreciation. Hamish Robinson, the retreat's director, was an entertaining, good-natured, and learned host; my time at Hawthornden was happy and productive.

I consulted many texts throughout the course of writing this one, but two in particular were hugely important—*How Dogs Think* by Dr. Stanley Coren, and *Walking the Appalachian Trail* by Larry Luxenberg. I also owe a debt of gratitude to my family and friends who helped with sections of the manuscript: Jon Raymond, Arthur Bradford, Cheston Knapp, Lance Cleland, Tony Perez, Ruta and Joseph Toutonghi. And, of course, ESSR.

For John and Ginny and Fields Marshall, my deepest thanks for letting me into their lives, and sharing their stories with me. For Bea and Phin—my sweet kids—thank you. And, for P.M.M.—what can I say? The adventure continues.